EDUCATION AND PHYSICAL EDUCATION

EDUCATION AND PHYSICAL EDUCATION

Editor

Shamshad Ahmed

ISHA BOOKS

Delhi-110033

Education and Physical Education

ISBN : 81-8205-236-X

Published in 2005 in India by
Isha Books
D-43, Prithviraj Road,
Adarsh Nagar, Delhi - 110033
e-mail : ishabooks@hotmail.com

Laser Typesetting at : Global Printers, New Delhi
Printed at : Chawla Offset Press, Delhi

Preface

Physical activity is critical to the development and maintenance of good health. The goal of physical education is to develop physically educated individuals who have the knowledge, skills, and confidence to enjoy a lifetime of healthful physical activity.

In most educational systems, physical education (PE) is a course which promotes physical activity and various sports. Physical education contributes, primarily through movement experiences, to the total growth and development of all children. Students have opportunities to gain knowledge, skills, and attitudes which promote physical activity as part of their everyday lives. Through regular participation in physical activity, students will have the opportunity to develop a pattern of life-enhancing and self-rewarding experiences that contribute to their potential to be healthier members of society. Students should be challenged to participate daily in healthy choices and health-enhancing activities and behaviours.

As an integral part of the educational process, physical education provides opportunities for students to participate in activities that promote wellness. Utilizing the strategies of problem solving, goal setting, and cooperative learning, physical education contributes to the understanding and knowledge of a healthy, active lifestyle, emphasizes safe and cooperative physical activity practices and contributes to an understanding of the consequences of substance abuse and to the practice and promotion of nonviolent physical activity. As a result of physical education, students are more likely to be better prepared as productive students, workers and contributors to their communities and organizations within society

Advances in technology applied in the physical education classroom provide a tool for instruction, assessment and record keeping. Technology offers the opportunity for advancement in instruction and enhanced student learning in physical education. The success of attaining physical education standards is directly related to student contact time, appropriate equipment, class size, and available facilities.

The present volume provides a comprehensive analysis of the nature, scope and trends of physical education. Its basic aim is to provide support and guidance for all related with physical education and to promote quality education and sports to all persons.

Editor

Contents

1

Meaning and Definition of Physical Education

Physical education is a component of education that takes place through movement. It creates the opportunity for individuals to learn and understand academic applications for healthy lives. In physical education, as in all academic areas, students must learn the basic skills which require practice and refinement in physical education settings. Students integrate and apply these skills in everyday life. Through regular participation in physical activity, students will have the opportunity to develop a pattern of life-enhancing and self-rewarding experiences that contribute to their potential to be healthier members of society. Students should be challenged to participate daily in healthy choices and health-enhancing activities and behaviours. Physical education and athletic programs have different purposes. The purpose of physical education is for all students:

— to learn and develop fundamental movement skills

— to become physically fit to participate regularly in physical activity

— to know the implications of and the benefits from involvement in physical activities, and

— to appreciate the value of physical activity and its contributions to a healthy lifestyle.

In contrast, athletic programs are essentially designed for students who desire to specialize in one or more sports and refine their talents in order to compete with others of similar interests and abilities. Developmentally appropriate physical education programs are designed for every child from the physically gifted to the physically challenged.

The intent is to provide students of all abilities and interests with a foundation of movement experiences that will eventually lead to active and healthy lifestyles. Physical education provides educational experiences that are movement based and that contribute to a student's comprehensive health status as well as other areas of academic performance and achievement. In US, federal legislation mandates that all children should have the right to participate in developmentally appropriate physical education activities, therefore, special populations should be recognized and their needs addressed.

Inclusion of physically and mentally challenged students creates special conditions in the physical education classroom. Adjustments in teaching strategies to educate students with challenging conditions must be expected and accepted as a variable which will influence student results. As an integral part of the educational process, physical education provides opportunities for students to participate in activities that promote wellness. Utilizing the strategies of problem solving, goal setting, and cooperative learning, physical education contributes to the understanding and knowledge of a healthy, active lifestyle, emphasizes safe and cooperative physical activity practices and contributes to an understanding of the consequences of substance abuse and to the practice and promotion of non-violent physical activity.

As a result of physical education, students are more likely to be better prepared as productive students, workers and contributors to their communities and organizations within society, as documented by the American Heart Association; the U.S Department of Health and Human Services, "A Report of the Surgeon General and the National Association for Sport and Physical Education (NASPE)."

Advances in technology applied in the physical education classroom provide a tool for instruction, assessment and record keeping. Technology offers the opportunity for advancement in instruction and enhanced student learning in physical education. The success of attaining physical education standards is directly related to student contact time, appropriate equipment, class size, and available facilities. Physical education can occur in a variety of environments such as the dance studio, swimming pool, gymnasium, field house, court, playing field, weight room, and out-of-doors. To ensure the competent delivery of safe physical education programs that are developmentally appropriate, standards should be administered by licensed physical education specialists.

Competent Skills in Physical Activities

As with all academic areas, basic skills are the foundation of a more active and productive life. The daily quality application of fundamental movement skills is the process by which we develop skillful movers. In order to meet this standard, the student will:

— demonstrate knowledge and application of fundamental movements skills: locomotor, non-locomotor and manipulative;

— move using the concepts from the movement framework — body, space, effort, and relationship;

— demonstrate competency in a variety of developmentally appropriate movement skills;

— apply movement skills to new activities and sports; and

— demonstrate the application of rules, strategies and behaviors in a variety of physical activity and sports.

In US, grades K-4, what students know and are able to do includes:

— demonstrating even rhythmic locomotor movements: walk, run, leap, hop, and jump and uneven rhythmic locomotor movements: gallop, slide and skip;

— demonstrating dynamic and static balance, with control, on a variety of moving and stationary objects or equipment;

— demonstrating mature patterns in the fundamental manipulative skills: throw, catch, kick, trap, roll, dribble, strike and volley;

— developing patterns and combinations of movement into repeatable sequences; and

— demonstrating the ability to change directions (dodge), transfer weight (feet to hands) and fall with control.

As students in grades 5-8 extend their knowledge, what they know and are able to do includes:

— incorporating basic defensive and offensive strategies in modified net games (e.g., tennis, volleyball, badminton) and invasive games (e.g., soccer, basketball);

— combining skills to competently participate in a variety of individual, team and dualsports (e.g., soccer, softball, tennis, track and field, team handball, field hockey and tumbling); and

— demonstrating one or more of the following dance or rhythmic activities: folk, square, social, creative, aerobic, modern, jazz, ballet and/or rhythmic activities such as rope jumping, lummi sticks and tinikling.

As students in grades 9-12 extend their knowledge, what they know and are able to do includes:

— demonstrating competency in one team-related activity or sport, through the execution of defensive and offensive strategies (e.g., soccer, softball, basketball, floor/field hockey, volleyball);

— demonstrating competency in one individual activity (e.g., aquatics, dance, gymnastics, golf, archery, adventure activities, and weight training); and

— demonstrating competency in one dual sport or game displaying an understanding of how it is played (e.g., tennis, badminton, racquetball, frisbee, handball).

Competency in Physical Fitness

Through regular participation in physical activity, students will develop appropriate levels of physical fitness. By obtaining and maintaining appropriate levels of fitness, students will be able to carry out daily tasks without undue fatigue, respond to emergency situations, and possess sufficient energy to enjoy active and productive lifestyles. In order to meet the standard, students will:

— develop health-related fitness: cardiovascular endurance, muscular endurance, muscular strength, flexibility and body composition;

— demonstrate competency in the following performance related or motor skill fitness components: agility, balance, coordination, power, reaction time, and speed;

— demonstrate an understanding that physical fitness is a part of a wellness program; and

— design and use personal fitness programs and appropriate technology to achieve and maintain physical fitness.

In grades K-4, what students know and are able to do includes:

— performing aerobic and anaerobic self-testing activities;

— maintaining appropriate body alignment while performing fitness activities; and

— controlling and supporting body weight in a variety of fitness activities.

As students in grades 5-8 extend their knowledge, what they know and are able to do includes:

— demonstrating various techniques, safety factors and knowledge required in a variety of muscular endurance and strength activities;

— participating in a variety of aerobic and anaerobic activities to attain cardiovascular endurance;

— demonstrating correct techniques for increasing and maintaining flexibility;

— demonstrating correct techniques for warming up and cooling down prior to and following aerobic and anaerobic exercise; and

— demonstrating how physical fitness increases wellness.

As students in grades 9-12 extend their knowledge, what they know and are able to do includes:

— sustaining and maintaining a moderate aerobic activity to achieve cardiovascular benefits;

— demonstrating principles of fitness development (overload, progression, specificity and individuality) in all areas of health-related fitness;

— demonstrating how to set goals for improvement in the areas of health-related fitness; and

— implementing and refining a personal fitness plan.

Knowledge Factors in Physical Activity

In order to meet this standard, students will:

— identify and describe the benefits, risks and safety factors associated with regular participation in physical activity;

— demonstrate knowledge that physical education activities such as dance, and sports come from a variety of cultural, historical, ethnic and national origins;

— demonstrate knowledge of rules, strategies and appropriate behaviors for selected physical activities;

— demonstrate knowledge of biomechanical principles that apply to the development of movement skills, for example, the analysis of a tennis swing or of shooting a basket;

— demonstrate the ability to set personal and group activity goals; and

— demonstrate the ability to set personal and group activity goals using appropriate technology.

The media and a variety of scientific sources report new evidence regarding the direct relationship between the comprehensive health of the student, the successful academic person and the quality producer in the work force. Therefore, in order to become a more active and productive citizen, the student must know how to make safe, healthy, and wise decisions about physical activity.

In grades K-4, what students know and are able to do includes:

— demonstrating knowledge of games, rules and sportsmanship;

— demonstrating knowledge of the fundamental components, strategies, equipment and technology used for participation in a variety of physical activities;

— describing the healthful benefits that result from regular and safe participation in physical activity;

— identifying the origins of physical education activities through low-organized games and dances representing a variety of ethnic cultures;

— demonstrating knowledge of the mature stage of fundamental movement skills; and

— designing games and movement sequences.

As students in grades 5-8 extend their knowledge, what they know and are able to do includes:

- — demonstrating an understanding of the negative effects of substance abuse on personal fitness and the performance of physical activities;
- — demonstrating an understanding of physiological and motor learning concepts during regular participation in physical activities;
- — developing and maintaining an individual plan of activity using appropriate technological advances;
- — demonstrating knowledge of the factors in both health-related and performance related fitness;
- — demonstrating knowledge of the roles of team members and officials in sports;
- — demonstrating knowledge of defensive and offensive strategies in lead-up games and sports;
- — demonstrating knowledge of complex movement skills used in physical activities;
- — identifying the influences of culture, ethnicity and history on dance, low organized and lead-up games, and other physical activities; and
- — detecting, analyzing, and correcting errors in personal performance.

As students in grades 9-12 extend their knowledge, what they know and are able to do includes:

- — demonstrating cooperative participation when engaged in competitive physical activities by following the rules and regulations specific to that activity;
- — identifying performance-related factors that contribute to participation in physical activity.
- — comparing and contrasting the strategies of defense and offense in various sports;
- — identifying and explaining the cultural, ethnic and historical roles of games, sports and dance;

— investigating the time, cost, available technology and participation requirements involved in a choice of physical activities;
— evaluating risks and safety factors that may affect physical activity throughout life; and
— analyzing biomechanical principles involved in sport to improve performance and reduce injury.

Physical Education in Primary School

The educational justification of physical education at the primary school level has been well promoted. It is evident that primary school students are at an optimal age in terms of motor skill learning, developing physical activity habits and for the formation of attitudes regarding physical activity and physical education. Although recognised as one of the most valuable and important vehicles for encouraging and teaching children to lead active lifestyles, primary school physical education is inhibited by low status, reduced time in the school curriculum, and poor quality programs.

Primary school physical education in Australia has suffered considerable criticism, with many doubts about the status of the subject and the quality of teaching. It appears that school physical education often fails to provide children with the opportunity to develop physical competencies and positive attitudes to physical activity. In many Australian primary schools, classroom teachers have total responsibility for the physical education instruction of their students. However, several Australian studies have described the lack of qualifications of classroom teachers to deliver physical education programs, largely as a result of inadequate teacher training in physical education.

Over the past 40 years, researchers have investigated whether differently trained teachers have similar success in the attainment of appropriate educational outcomes for primary physical education programs. In general, literature has supported the conclusion that primary school children taught by physical education specialists demonstrate significantly better levels of achievement in most outcome measures than those who are taught by non-specialists. For example, superior scores for specialist-taught students are evident in motor performance, academic achievement, fitness levels, physical activity levels, and attitudes to physical activity.

Some researchers have indicated that specialists display more effective teaching behaviours than non-specialists. The educational argument against the employment of specialist physical education teachers rests largely on the premise that a one teacher per class model allows a holistic delivery of the curriculum and caters for the individual needs of students. Some studies have reported favourable results for non-specialists in terms of feelings about physical education, beliefs about the purposes of elementary physical education, and in improving physical education teaching credentials.

As an alternative to the highly costly proposal of employing specialist physical education teachers in primary schools, several studies have shown that generalist teachers can improve the quality of their physical education lessons with regular training and assistance from specialists. Regardless of whether a specialist or non-specialist is responsible for teaching physical education, it is imperative that qualified and competent teachers teach physical education, given the potential benefit to students of involvement in physical education programs.

Many classroom teachers consider themselves unqualified to teach physical education, and recognise a number of barriers, which inhibit their ability to effectively teach physical education. Some of the major barriers commonly discussed include inadequate facilities and equipment, feelings of inadequacy, low levels of confidence, and lack of time and interest. Aside from inadequate facilities and equipment, most of these barriers are linked to a teacher's attitudes and beliefs regarding physical education.

Attitudinal Disposition of the Primary School Teacher

The investigation of the attitudinal disposition of prospective and practising preservice teachers may improve understanding of their perceptions of physical education, their willingness to teach physical education, and how confident they are in their ability to affect student learning in physical education. The logical assumption is that more favourable levels of outcome attainment will be realised by students if they experience lessons implemented by competent and confident teachers who are committed to teaching physical education.

The teacher's affective disposition may have a profound affect on a student's attitude to physical education and subsequently exert a significant influence on a pupil's physical education experience. Smith reported that the attitude of the teacher was one of the most vital factors in the success of primary physical education programs. Some researchers have found that many non-specialist teachers hold negative attitudes towards physical education, and question its value for children.

Some more recent studies have attempted to investigate these areas, but further research is necessary to investigate the attitudinal disposition of non-specialists and specialists and to compare results for different groups of preservice and inservice teachers. Xiang et al. examined the attitudinal disposition and beliefs of preservice classroom teachers before and after a fields-based course using two open-ended questions. After this course, half of the preservice classroom teachers indicated that they were not willing to teach physical education.

Xiang et al. found that many classroom teachers recognised that they were not equipped to teach physical education after observing the complex nature of physical education teaching. It is important that the attitudinal disposition of teachers is acknowledged in the development of appropriate physical education teacher education courses, as preservice teachers' views about physical education may need to be challenged or complemented. Many researchers have indicated that early school experiences in physical education provide prospective teachers with a large range of information about physical education, which may potentially affect attitudes, beliefs, and teaching practices. Some argues that preservice teachers' beliefs about physical education, developed during their personal school experiences in physical education, act and persist as a reference point which is used against any different theories they come across during preservice training.

It is well recognised in the literature that teacher educators encounter resistance from students who have been 'socialised' into teaching as a result of their schooling experiences. Subsequently, the influence of teacher education is questioned, as school socialisation agencies are often much stronger than preservice teacher training. A variety of studies have consistently testified that teachers' prior experiences are so powerful that preservice training may have little effect on their beliefs, particularly if they contradict already established beliefs.

Some researchers in physical education have provided evidence that ideologies or beliefs may change as a result of field experiences or throughout teacher training. Other researchers have noted the positive effect of tertiary training on preservice teachers' attitudes to physical education, attitudes to physical activity, and attitudes to movement education. Some researchers have suggested that many of the effects of teacher education on attitudes and beliefs are only temporary Some described how beginning teachers leave behind innovative teaching strategies and improved attitudes developed during teacher training, as they are socialised into the teaching profession. This 'wash out' effect has also been identified with beginning physical education teachers.

Adults and Teens Attitude Towards Physical Education

in US, the National Association for Sport and Physical Education (NASPE), a nonprofit membership organization of over 25,000 professionals in the fitness and physical activity fields, is the only national association dedicated to strengthening basic knowledge about sport and physical education among professionals and the general public. Putting that knowledge into action in schools and communities across the nation is critical to improved academic performance, social reform and the health of individuals. NASPE is an association of the American Alliance for Health, Physical Education, Recreation and Dance (AAHPERD). NASPE wanted to go directly to adults and teens to better understand their beliefs about physical education, physical activity and nutrition.

Adults and teens have similar attitudes toward physical education.

— 81% of adults believe that "daily physical education should be mandatory in schools." Nearly three-quarters (71%) of teens agree.

— The majority of adults and teens strongly agree that "physical education helps children prepare to become active, healthy adults" (Adults-64% Teens- 54%) and "helps children build social skills as well as physical strength and coordination" (Adults-64% Teens-53%). In fact, almost half (46%) of the adults strongly agree that participating in physical education as a child helped them to become active, healthy adults.

Frequency of Physical Education Classes

— 56% of adults with children in the household (aged 6-17) say that their child does not have physical education class daily. 47% of teens say they do not have daily physical education class.

— About half (48%) of teens believe that they have the right amount of physical education classes. Two out of five teens (42%) say they would take physical education classes more if available, and only 9% would take them less often than they currently do.

Physical Education Class and Child's Academic Needs

— The vast majority (91%) of American adults who have children in the household (aged 6-17) believe that physical education class does not interfere with children's academic needs.

— Less than one-quarter of adults and teens feel that "children should concentrate on academic subjects at school, and leave the physical activities for after school" (Adults-15% Teens-21%). Parents and teens are not concerned that "physical education classes in schools are dangerous" (Adults-90% Teens-94%).

— Most adults and teens strongly believe that "participation in team sports helps children learn lessons about discipline and teamwork that are important and will help them in the future" (Adults-67% Teens-69%).

What Students Like/Dislike about Physical Education

— When asked to name what they like about physical education class, teens top mentions are: the opportunity to have exercise (20%), getting fit (18%), it's fun (16%) and the activities offered (16%). Only 5% said they don't like anything about it.

— Teens' top mentions for things they dislike are: running (13%), boring activities (no variety) (9%), and dressing/ undressing for class (7%).

Learning in Physical Education Class

— When asked to name what teens think they should be learning in physical education class, half (52%) responded that they should be learning how to stay fit. Other top mentions included learning skills and rules for different physical activities (20%) and learning how their body works (10%).

Adult Physical Activity

Getting enough physical activity to maintain a healthy lifestyle: The majority of adults (60%) feel that they are getting enough physical activity to maintain a healthy lifestyle. (The U.S. Surgeon General's Report on Physical Activity and Health, 1996, the most prominent piece of public information concerning physical activity up to that time, reported that 60% are not getting enough physical activity.)

Things which prevent adults from getting enough physical activity: Those who do believe they're not getting enough physical activity say it's because of their job (33%), lack of interest or motivation (27%), not having enough time (19%) or health problems (13%). Adults with children in a household also indicate that childcare is a barrier to getting more physical activity.

Weekly Exercise: Nearly three quarters of American adults report getting at least some exercise for a period of at least 30 minutes per week, with an average of 3.8 times a week. Men, those who are younger, those with some college education or more and those who participated in interscholastic sports as a child are more likely to report getting some weekly exercise.

Importance of child being physically dit: Not surprisingly, nearly all (99%) adults with children in the household (aged 6-17) feel that it is important for the child to be physically fit, with 80% believing this to be extremely important.

Daily Physical Activity of Child: Americans with children in the household report that their child spends an average of 1.2 hours daily doing physical activities, not including physical education class. Adults with children in the household reported the top activities outside of school for their children are basketball (24%), baseball/softball (19%), bicycling (11%), soccer (10%), football (9%) and swimming (9%).

Setting limits on time children spend on activities: The majority of adults report that they set limits on the time their children spend doing certain activities, such as playing video games or playing on the computer (59%) and television watching (57%). Less than half (41%) attempt to control time spent on other non-homework related activities.

Most teens ages 12-17 (79%) say that they eat a balanced diet that includes grains, fruits, vegetables, dairy, proteins, fats or oils and sweets. Younger teens (aged 12-14) are slightly more likely than those ages 15-17 to report they eat a balanced diet (83% vs. 75%). Two out of three teens (67%) report participation in a team sport at school. The top sports participated in are: basketball (23%), baseball/softball (17%), football (15%), track and field (13%), soccer (12%) and volleyball (11%). When asked to name the physical activities offered in school physical education which they like the most, teens' top mentions are: basketball (34%), football (17%), volleyball (14%), soccer (13%), baseball/softball (13%) and track and field (10%).

The majority (69%) of Americans with children in the household believe their children are fit, with one-quarter (28%) seeing them as extremely fit. By comparison, only half (54%) of teens ages 12-17 believe that they, are fit, with only 12% viewing themselves as extremely fit. Adults with children in the household believe that their children are not fit primarily because of lack of interest or motivation (24%), not enough time (13%) and watching television (13%). On the other hand, teens who believe they aren't fit mention not having enough time (24%), doing homework (19%), and lack of interest or motivation (13%) as the main deterrents to their getting more physical activity. Overall, adults tend to feel that the child doesn't get enough physical activity because he/she lacks interest or motivation while teens tend to feel they just don't have enough time for physical activity due to homework or other things.

Nearly all (99%) adults think that proper hydration is extremely or somewhat important to maintaining good health, with most (88%) seeing this as extremely important. Similarly, nearly all (98%) teens ages 12-17 view proper hydration as extremely or somewhat important to maintaining good health, but with much less (58%) thinking it is extremely important.

American adults report consuming an average of 8.7 eight-ounce glasses of liquid in a normal day. Teens (ages 12-17) report slightly less—7.0 eightounce glasses of liquid daily. The majority of adults (59%) say water is their favorite thirst quencher. Other beverages mentioned are: soft drinks (16%), fruit juice (8%), iced tea (5%) and sports drinks (3%). Teens primarily choose water (38%) and soft drinks (23%) as well as fruit juice (19%), sports drinks (8%) and milk (8%). Among adults, those 55 years and over who get some weekly exercise are more likely than other adults to say water is their favorite thirst quencher (66% versus 57%).

Effective Physical Education Programme

The effective physical education programme has clear expectations for student learning that are specifically defined in writing for each grade level. The effective physical education program has high and clear expectations for what students are expected to know and be able to do. Motor skill, cognitive, affective and fitness outcomes are defined specifically for all grade levels and are consistent with the state standards. The effective physical education program has a written curriculum to achieve the outcomes defined in the curriculum. This written curriculm should:

— reflect the state standards,

— be coordinated at the district level preK–12,

— include a statement of philosophy,

— include clearly defined performance standards for all age levels,

— include suggested scope and sequence of learning experiences,

— include a description of how each performance standard is to be assessed,

— be used to plan instruction,

— be revisited on a regular basis; and

— be distributed to all teachers who teach physical education.

The effective physical education program takes a lifespan approach to the development of standards. The current and long-term needs of students are considered in the development of skills, fitness, attitudes, and values toward physical activity. The motor content of the effective program is consistent with "best practice" as defined by the local curriculum guide

Primary School

The curriculum for the primary school includes body management, manipulative and game skills, educational dance, and fitness.

Middle School

The curriculum at the middle school includes opportunities for students to become proficient in a wide variety of movement forms (net/racket, target, team, outdoor pursuits, individual, and dance) at modified levels of skill and complexity and to acquire beginning knowledge related to assessing and developing personal fitness programs.

High School

The curriculum at the high school provides opportunities for students to become competent and proficient in several movement forms (net/racket, target, team, outdoor pursuits, individual, and dance) elected from a variety of choices. In the high school curriculum, students will also be able to design and develop a personalized physical fitness program, participate regularly in health-enhancing physical activity beyond the physical education class, and meet the gender and age group health-related physical fitness standards.

The effective physical education program addresses both the cognitive and the affective dimensions of learning, directly and specifically as content and indirectly as products of processes. Both affective learning and cognitive learning are the product of the teacher's methods and approaches to teaching content and definitive learning experiences designed for specific outcomes in these domains.

The curriculum of the effective physical education program is designed to be developmentally appropriate for each grade level including students with special needs. The curriculum should differentiate among the grade levels. A clear developmental sequence should be evident throughout the planned preK-12 curriculum. The curriculum of the effective physical education program is integrated into and coordinated with the school curriculum rather than existing apart from it. School and district policy and goals are reflected in the physical education curriculum. The goals of the physical education program are reflected in school and district goals and planning materials.

The effective physical education program is developed with and shared with the community. The curriculum as a whole is approved by the school board, and the standards are shared with the community.

The curriculum of the effective physical education program includes clear strategies and materials for student assessment and program assessment. Decisions as to how students will be assessed and how the program will be evaluated on a regular basis should be included in the curriculum.

The curriculum of the effective physical education program offers opportunities for participation and encourages students to participate in physical activities beyond the required physical education program available to all students. These are a few examples of additional physical activities in which students may become involved:

- youth leagues, church leagues,
- community recreation,
- YMCA programs,
- intramurals,
- early-morning/after-school programs, and
- field days.

Effective Instruction in Physical Education

Effective instruction in physical education provides students with educationally rich learning experiences that:

- have the potential to improve motor performance,
- are rich in affective and cognitive content,
- provide maximum participation, and
- are appropriate to the age and level of development of each learner.

Effective instruction in physical education is planned to help students reach specific learning outcomes that are both consistent with the curriculum and developmentally appropriate for all students, including those with special needs:

- The teacher has a written plan for each lesson.
- Plans are written separately for different developmental levels.
- Written plans include specific learning objectives, learning experiences, and assessment criteria and procedures.
- Individualized Education Plans (IEPs) are written for each student with special needs.

Effective instruction in physical education establishes and maintains a positive learning environment with clear and shared expectations and consequences:

— Off-task or inappropriate behavior is at a minimum.

— The teacher has clear expectations for student learning.

— Expectations for appropriate behavior and consequences for inappropriate behavior are shared with students and are reinforced.

— Students can work independently as well as cooperatively in a focused manner.

— The teacher in an effective instructional environment in physical education presents and communicates tasks to learners effectively and accurately.

Effective instruction in physical education develops content in a manner that gradually leads the learner to increasing levels of ability with the content:

— Content development in instruction includes refining, extension, and application/assessment tasks.

— Content is developed so students can be successful and see improvement.

Learning experiences are modified appropriately to increase or decrease difficulty on an individual basis so that the proper level of challenge and success is provided for all students.

Effective instruction in physical education provides a maximum opportunity to learn:

— Content is chosen and developed to provide maximum practice time with the intended learning.

— Students are organized into groups to provide maximum practice.

— Sufficient equipment is available for maximum practice.

- The teacher manages instruction so that he or she spendsas little time as possible on organization.
- The teacher uses all available time for instructional purposes.

Effective instruction in physical education uses a variety of instructional strategies:

- Direct and indirect teaching strategies are used.
- Teacher-centered and student-centered strategies are used.
- Different delivery systems for instruction are used (e.g., station teaching, interactive teaching, peer teaching).

Effective instruction in physical education maintains a physically and psychologically safe environment for students:

- The teacher arranges facilities and instructional equipment for safe participation.
- The teacher teaches students how to participate safely and reinforces safe participation.
- The teacher creates a supportive social and interactive environment for all students.
- The teacher creates opportunities for all students to experience success and challenge.

Effective instruction in physical education incorporates assessment experiences into instruction:

- The teacher shares expectations with students prior to instruction.
- Formative assessment is used to provide students and the teacher with information on student progress.
- Informal application/assessment experiences are designed as part of the development of content with students.

Organizational and Administrative Aspects of Physical Education Programme

Scheduling

All students should have daily physical education throughout preK-12. All students at the preschool, elementary, and middle school level should participate in an instructional program of physical education on a daily basis. Throughout the high school level, students should have the opportunity to participate in physical education in a scheduling format equivalent to other subject areas. The needs of students and not the needs of teachers determine the class time allocated for daily physical education. With some flexibility for content and daily situations, the following durations of a class period are appropriate for students of different age levels:

— 20 minutes preschool

— 25 minutes early elementary

— 30-45 minutes upper elementary

— 50-60 minutes middle school

— 50-90 minutes high school

Physical education is scheduled so that the objectives of the program are supported:

— The ratio of students to teacher in any single physical education class is no greater than the ratio in other academic classes.

— Team teaching is considered an occasion to enhance opportunities for student learning and not to reduce the instructional responsibilities of the teacher.

— The use of itinerant teachers in a school and district should be limited.

— Students are not allowed to substitute other curricular or extracurricular activities for the required physical education program.

The placement of students with special needs is considered in terms of the least restrictive environment and the needs of all students within the school. In US, federal 504 plans include physical education, and physical education teachers write the IEPs for students with special needs. A master schedule of teaching stations, as well as faculty and class assignments, is available.

Policies and Procedures

Policies and procedures that support the program are established and distributed in clear written form:

— Mechanisms for communication with school administration about the physical education program are in place.

— Procedures for emergencies have been established and are shared in written form with all faculty and students.

— Established policies and practices give physical education classes priority over the use of physical education facilities.

— The physical education program is a part of the strategic planning of the school.

Clear policies for grading students as well as excusing students from physical activity or class are established and circulated in clear written form:

— Students are graded on the achievement of program objectives.

— It is rare that students who are healthy enough to come to school are not healthy enough to participate in physical education.

Faculty of Physical Education

All faculty are certified to teach physical education in South Carolina. The teaching load of each teacher is commensurate with the loads of other teachers in the school and reflects the additional responsibilities of the teacher. The primary responsibility of the faculty is to teach and not to coach. Teachers who also coach or perform other extracurricular duties are held accountable for their teaching. Teachers who also coach are given adequate release-time from their teaching responsibilities so that they are able to perform both teaching and coaching jobs effectively.

Faculty are expected to maintain and upgrade their skills and are supported in their efforts at professional growth. Professional growth is a part of the short-term and long-term plans of the school. The school/district provides teachers with opportunities to improve their skills through financial compensation, travel funds, and substitute availability. Faculty are active in improving their professional competence in teaching physical education and are involved in at least some of the following pursuits on a regular basis:

— attending district in-service programs,

— participating in SCAHPERD programs and learning opportunities,

— continuing to take course work,

— attending professional physical education conferences and/or meetings,

— visiting model/demonstration schools, and

— obtaining additional endorsements

— faculty are evaluated on a regular basis.

Faculty assessment is part of a planned teacher development program designed to hold teachers accountable for effective teaching practices as well as to contribute to their professional growth. Assessment should be done by an observer with a clear notion of effective teaching in physical education, using criteria specific to the field of physical education.

Facilities and Equipment

Adequate equipment and appropriate facilities are provided to implement the curriculum:

— An adequate budget for physical education is provided on a yearly basis apart from the athletic program.

— An adequate number of indoor and outdoor teaching stations are available for the number of students.

— Classroom space is available for high school physical education programs (fitness instruction, viewing videotapes).

— Equipment and facilities are clean and safe and are inspected on a regular basis.

The Model Lesson

Teachers create an optimal learning environment and an effective learning experience for their students through careful planning. The heart of effective instruction is the actual physical education lesson. Throughout the lesson the teacher should maintain an orderly, safe, businesslike atmosphere and have clear expectations for the behavior and achievement of students. The teacher implements the lesson plan and makes adjustments as necessary for students not experiencing success or not participating. Each day should begin with a variety of warm-up exercises involving the muscles to be used in the instructional phase and lasting one or two minutes. All students should be expected to perform the exercises to the best of their ability. However, adjustments may need to be made to deal with individual abilities. The teacher supervises the students, explains the purpose of each exercise, and provides corrective or positive feedback.

Warm-up is followed by the instructional phase. At this point the teacher explains the purpose of the main activity, which will include demonstrations and explanations. Then comes the activity phase. During the activity phase each student is engaged in the skill-learning time, with enough correct practice trials being provided during class time to acquire the desired skill. Activities should be designed to keep to a minimum the amount of time spent waiting in line and moving between activities. Equipment should be deployed efficiently (at least one object for every two students). Whenever possible, students should be placed in cooperative learning groups. When working with individual students, the teacher should personalize instruction by using the student's name and giving feedback equally to boys and girls and to high achievers and low achievers in appropriate ways. At the end of the class, the teacher should provide a chance for discussion or processing of the lesson, encouraging the students to review the objectives or key points. In this way students can see relationships, attitudes, values, and other insights related to the lesson, and teachers can adjust the lessons for optimal learning the next day.

Sample Model Lesson:

— Elementary

— Middle School

— High School

Variety of Strategies

Teachers should use a variety of teaching styles, including teacher-directed and student-initiated learning, to satisfy the learning styles of individual students and stimulate higher levels of thinking and creativity. Teaching styles might include command, practice, self-check, guided discovery, student-designed and student-initiated teaching, and self-teaching. Teachers should also employ a variety of instructional approaches, including competency-based learning, contract learning, drill, information processing, lecture, mastery learning, programmed instruction, and role-playing.

Especially appropriate for physical education instruction is cooperative learning. Assigning students to small learning groups (three to six members each) allows teachers and students to achieve a variety of goals, both social and cognitive. In addition, research has shown that cooperative learning produces higher achievement; improves cross-ethnic friendships and social skills; enhances self-image; and promotes greater interdependence, improved role-taking abilities (e.g., leadership), and a better classroom climate.

The first step in cooperative learning is the formation of heterogeneous teams. The size of each team will vary according to the activity; however, groups of three to six students (mixed as to ability, race, and gender) have proven to be most successful. After the teams have been formed, students need activities for team building and time to practice and receive feedback on appropriate social skills. The specifics of cooperative learning lessons depend to a great extent on which method among many different cooperative learning approaches is chosen. However, the teacher must ensure positive interdependence and both individual and group rewards. A team can succeed only if all members are interdependent in their contributions toward a common goal.

Instructional strategies for special needs

Every physical education class include students who are high achievers; those who are low achievers; and those, the majority, in the middle. Effective instructional strategies take into account the diverse needs of what are often very heterogeneous groups. All students, not just a select few, should receive positive feedback and reinforcement from the instructor or other students; and all should have opportunities to be involved.

Gender equity

American federal law and California law require that students of both sexes be treated equally in integrated physical education classes. All students, male and female, should be given the teacher's attention and feedback on an equal basis and should be called on equally to demonstrate new skills. The teacher should also discipline males and females equally.

Differences in language or communication

Different types of instructional approaches will also be needed for students with limited proficiency in English or other communication problems. Bilingual interpreters or instructors skilled in sign language may be needed. For non-English speakers, information offered in their native language helps develop not just understanding but a positive attitude toward the information.

For teachers who do not speak a second language and for students who are limited-English proficient, sheltered instruction is another approach that can be used. Sheltered instruction provides students with a variety of interactive and multimodal means to accessing information. In sheltered instruction the language demands of the lesson can be modified through such techniques as clear enunciation, controlled vocabulary, fewer idioms, and such contextual cues as gestures, facial expressions, demonstrations, props, visuals, and overhead transparencies. Cooperative learning has also proved effective in teaching students at various levels of English proficiency because high levels of interaction are associated with enhanced learning of content and English.

Instructional materials

Support should include films, filmstrips, videos, laser disks, textbooks, overhead projectors, heart monitors, camcorder, video cameras, and computers. There are many physical educators using technology around the state and world. For more assistance in learning to use these materials and other new instructional strategies consult professional resources.There are a variety of vendors where you can order these materials.

2

Aims and Objectives

Physical education is a necessity for the health and well-being of every student. As a unique and essential part of the total education program, physical education can significantly enhance all aspects of development including health, physical fitness, movement knowledge, academic performance, goal setting, self-esteem, stress management, and social skills. Evidence continues to mount that regular physical activity can prevent and manage coronary heart disease, which is the leading cause of death and disability in the United States. Unfortunately, few Americans engage in regular physical activity, despite the benefits. Research findings clearly demonstrate that daily exercise, from early childhood throughout life, is a primary factor in maintaining health and enriching the quality of life. People begin to acquire and establish patterns of health-related behavior during childhood and adolescence. Schools are an efficient vehicle for providing this physical education instruction.

Although many students participate in extra-curricular athletics, and these programs may meet the movement and exercise needs of the participants during their season of competition, such programs do not accommodate all students. Therefore, that physical education is an integral part of a comprehensive education and must be included on a daily basis. Finally, it should be understood that quality physical education is predicated upon having competent, dedicated, and knowledgeable teachers who utilize appropriate instructional techniques, strategies, and assessments.

Development and Implementation of Quality Physical Education Instruction

Educators are committed to the development and implementation of quality physical education instruction. *Moving Into the Future - National Physical Education Standards: A Guide to Content and Assessment*, a book developed by the US National Association for Sport and Physical Education, should be used as the guide to the delivery of KPBSD physical education programs. The following content standards in physical education, which identify what a student should know or be able to do, will be applied to instruction at all grade levels.

A Physically Educated Person:

1. Demonstrates competency in many movement forms and proficiency in a few movement forms. (Motor Skills)
2. Applies movement concepts and principles to the learning and development of motor skills. (Application)
3. Exhibits a physically active lifestyle. (Active Living)
4. Achieves and maintains a health-enhancing level of fitness. (Physical Fitness)
5. Demonstrates responsible personal and social behavior in physical activity settings. (Personal and Social Skills)
6. Demonstrates understanding and respect for differences among people in physical activity settings. (Cooperation)
7. Understands that physical activity provides opportunities for enjoyment, challenge, self-expression, and social interaction. (Values Physical Activity)

Elementary physical education program

The focus of the elementary physical education program is the introduction and exploration of physical education skills and concepts. As an important part of the elementary school program that uniquely contributes to the school's overall goals, physical education emphasizes the total development of the child (i.e. physical, motor, cognitive, social, and emotional development). It is critical at the elementary level that students be guided through a series of developmentally appropriate experiences and activities that promote a desire to engage in physical activities, promote a sense of self worth, encourage cooperation, and self control, and lead to choices that promote a healthy life style.

To deliver a quality elementary physical education program, 90-120 minutes of instruction per week is recommended. This instruction is to include vigorous physical activity, diagnosis and learning of neuromuscular skills, information about physical activity and fitness, and time to enjoy the use of skills and knowledge. Even though recess is an important part of an elementary school, it should not be used as a substitute for physical education instruction.

Middle School physical education program

The focus of the middle school physical education program is to provide a daily opportunity for students to participate in a wide variety of physical activities and experiences that promote the mastery of the core skills introduced at the elementary level. Middle school physical education will build a framework for lifetime activities and healthy living. Middle school is a time of transition, which may bring about an upheaval in physical, emotional, social, and intellectual worlds. To successfully bridge this transition, students will explore and apply information, as well as participate in activities that empower them to assume responsibility for their own lifetime health, wellness, and fitness.

High School physical education program

The focus of the high school physical education program is to promote healthy living and knowledge of lifetime activities.

The student will take the responsibility for and apply their learning to their personal lifetime health and wellness. All students are required to take a one semester Lifetime Activities and Healthy Living course in the 9-10th grade year. To meet the US, National Standards and benchmarks and make fitness for life a priority, a minimum of two credits of physical education throughout their high school experience is recommended. Current KPBSD graduation requirements include one credit of physical education.

Lifetime Activities of Physical Education

The elective activities of Physical Education are chosen for their unique contribution to the development of a well-rounded student. The particular activity is not the end goal, but is the vehicle through which a mindset of lifetime fitness is instilled. Rather than have a separate course for each individual activity, three courses are available which encompass all. In this standards based curriculum, the standards are set forth and the teacher chooses the activities that will be used in the course to meet the standards. The three courses available are:

— Movement and Activity

— Physical Training

— Individual/Dual/Team Activities

This course is designed to introduce and provide opportunities for all students to participate in a wide variety of activities to enhance fitness through various movement forms. This course emphasizes self-improvement and further development of individual skills leading to lifetime personal fitness. These activities will enhance the student's knowledge of physiology, endurance, and strength development. The emphasis in this course is to continue conditioning, refine skills, and become proficient in a variety of recreational activities, whereby the student will continue these activities past his/her high school years.

Comprehensive Helath Education and Physical Education

School failure is often a symptom of competing issues and problems that overwhelm a student's life. Poor nutrition, lack of sleep, chronic or untreated illness, pregnancy, a disorganized home, substance abuse, or a threatening environment may all contribute to a student's inability to cope with the rigorous demands of learning. Poor health in all its dimensions clearly interferes with school performance. Young people from all social and economic levels may experience these problems that compete for their time, energy, and commitment. While most children and adolescents are considered healthy using traditional health markers such as disease patterns, an even more deadly pattern is emerging.

Young males, across all races and age groups, are dying at a consistently higher rate than young females. Why? Most of these needless tragedies are the direct result of poor choices resulting in substance use, homicide, or motor vehicle crashes involving the use of alcohol. These tragedies are preventable. Preventing health-threatening behaviors and instituting health-enhancing ones are crucial to the prevention of needless death and despair. Empowering young people to make lifeenhancing decisions enables them to engage in the work of youth-learning.

According to John Seffrin, chief executive officer of the American Cancer Society, human health is both an end and a means to an end. For this reason, Dr. Seffrin defines school health education as education in the art of living. Good health is necessary for effective learning. Feeling physically and mentally healthy is essential as students face intense competition, peer and media pressure, and the stresses of daily physical, emotional, social, intellectual, and work-related activities. Business and community leaders now recognize the need for a healthy, productive workforce armed with critical-thinking skills, problem-solving skills, cooperative and collaborative qualities, self-management skills, and finely-tuned communication skills.

Many businesses offer employee wellness programs including fitness programs, preventive healthcare, and occupational services to ensure the health and productivity of their employees. Comprehensive health education and physical education play important roles in the development of citizens who are able to form healthy relationships, use social skills appropriately, demonstrate a sense of intellectual curiosity, and practice health-enhancing behaviors in preparation for their role as well-educated, productive citizens.

The Comprehensive Health Education and Physical Education Core Curriculum Content Standards address the greatest threats to morbidity and mortality. In adults, three major causes contribute to twothirds of all mortality and a great amount of morbidity, suffering, and healthcare costs. According to a 1997 report issued by the Centers for Disease Control and Prevention (CDC), the use of tobacco products, the consumption of an unhealthy diet, and a daily pattern of inactivity contribute to India's battle with heart disease, stroke, and cancer. Significantly, adolescents account for one quarter of all new HIV infections, one quarter of all new sexually transmitted diseases (STDs), and approximately one million pregnancies per year. The leading causes of death in our young people involve intentional and unintentional injuries such as motor vehicle crashes (with one half of those being alcohol related), homicide, and suicide.

Clearly, our greatest health challenges are critically linked to the health-related behaviors individuals have chosen to adopt. While multiple factors (including heredity and environment) account for a percentage of premature illness and death, lifestyle choices contribute to over 50% of such morbidity and mortality. Complicating this scenario is the simple fact that poor health choices do not generally occur in isolation; that is, these behaviors cluster in predictable ways and follow a developmental progression. These facts are not new.

Throughout history scientists, physicians, philosophers, and educators have promoted the "laws of health." The ancient

Greeks, known for their commitment to preventive medicine and fitness, believed that "Eating alone will not keep a man well; he must also take exercise. For food and exercise, while possessing opposite qualities, yet work together to produce health". Greek citizens were advised to breathe fresh air, eat proper food, drink the right beverages, get plenty of sleep, and consider their emotions as part of overall well-being.

After World War I, many states mandated health, safety, and physical education for public school students. The New Jersey mandate, was initiated to better prepare young men for the rigors of military service. Since that time, family life education, HIV/AIDS prevention education, and substance abuse education have been added to the original requirement. In addition, numerous statutes require instruction in specific issues such as Lyme disease, sexual assault prevention, fire safety, or cancer awareness. The content of physical education programs has not been so clearly delineated in New Jersey statutes or regulations.

Comprehensive health education and physical education are complementary disciplines, sharing a similar yet distinct body of knowledge. The Comprehensive Health Education and Physical Education Standards provide a consolidated approach to instruction with wellness as the common theme. The aim of the Standards is to enable students to take responsibility for their actions using sound, informed judgment while considering the impact of those actions for themselves, for their family, and for society at large.

For every dollar spent on high-quality, multicomponent school health education, society saves $13 in direct costs (e.g., medical treatment for preventable disease, addiction counseling, alcohol-related motor vehicle crashes, drug-related crime). This includes the indirect costs of lost productivity due to premature death and the social welfare expenditures associated with adolescent pregnancy. Comprehensive health education and physical education aim to address these serious impediments to school completion, self-efficacy, and wellness. If the purpose of education is to prepare young people for their place in our complex and fast-paced world, then comprehensive health education and physical education-education in the art of living-are significant parts of that preparation.

According to Maurice Elias, Ph.D, professor of psychology at Rutgers University and colleagues, schools and communities need to do more to prepare young people for the challenges and demands of life. Their research supports school-based programs that promote social and emotional health as well as physical health. Comprehensive health education and physical education aim to provide students with the knowledge and skills to meet those demands.

Benefits of Comprehensive Health Education and Physical Education

Comprehensive health education and physical education:

— Empower students to make informed decisions about issues that impact their present health, the health of their family and friends, and the health of society at-large.

— Enable students to enact health-enhancing behaviors before damaging patterns are firmly established.

— Enhance students' ability to become cautious and competent consumers.

— Strengthen students' ability to recognize, analyze, and react to unhealthy or dangerous situations in a safe and appropriate manner.

— Strengthen students' ability to focus on learning, academic achievement, and preparation for the world of work.

— Empower students to navigate through and around conflicting messages, risky behaviors, and mounting pressures and to develop dependable support systems.

— Assist students to recognize, understand, and address immediate or chronic health problems in order to prevent long-term health problems.

— Empower students to choose lifetime physical activities that they enjoy and have confidence in.

— Enable students to participate in lifetime activities that promote, support, and maintain wellness.

Coordinated School Health Programmes

Comprehensive health education and physical education are two components of a nationally recognized model, endorsed by the CDC, that supports and promotes student, school, family, and community wellness. Coordinated school health programs (formerly called comprehensive school health programs) feature eight components that provide a framework for the requisite programs and services shown to promote healthy behavior, promote school attendance and student achievement, and foster environments conducive to school completion.

Comprehensive health education and physical education are best delivered within the context of a coordinated program that includes all eight elements, linked by a common network and philosophy. Schools with coordinated and comprehensive programs in place are considered health-promoting environments. Coordinated school health programs include:

— Policies and procedures that support and reinforce classroom instruction. Health messages are clear and consistent.

— Access to health services and referrals to community healthcare providers. Classroom instructors, school nurses, parents, and community healthcare providers work as a team to support student health.

— In-school support and referral for those needing counseling services. Classroom instructors and school counselors work in concert with social workers and mental health specialists to provide immediate care in time of crisis and to facilitate long-term care for those who need it.

— A safe school environment. School staff work to provide a clean, safe, drug-free and weaponfree environment.

— Nutritious and appealing food choices. The food services staff provides meals that reflect the tenets of sound nutrition yet are appealing to young people.

— School staff that promote and support wellness. School staff members are supported in their own efforts to achieve health and well-being.

— Parental and community support. Schools involve parents and community members in health promotion efforts and policy making.

Coordinated school health programs are an integral part of school reform efforts. These programs reflect a collaborative school community seeking to enhance the health and well-being of its members. Instructional programs grounded in a health-promoting environment tend to be more successful, mo reconsistent, and more effective. According to the CDC, a coordinated school health program includes:

Health Education: A planned, sequential, K-12 curriculum that addresses the physical, mental, emotional, and social dimensions of health. The curriculum is designed to motivate and assist students to maintain and improve their health, prevent disease, and reduce health-related risk behaviors. It allows students to develop and demonstrate increasingly sophisticated health-related knowledge, attitudes, skills, and practices. The comprehensive curriculum includes a variety of topics such as personal health, family health, community health, consumer health, environmental health, sexuality education, mental and emotional health, injury prevention and safety, nutrition, prevention and control of disease, and substance use and abuse. Qualified, trained teachers provide health education.

Physical Education: A planned, sequential K-12 curriculum that provides cognitive content and learning experiences in a variety of activity areas such as basic movement skills; physical fitness; rhythm and dance; games; team, dual, and individual sports; tumbling and gymnastics; and aquatics. Quality physical education should promote, through a variety of planned physical activities, each student's optimum physical, mental, emotional, and social development and should promote activities and sports that all students enjoy and can pursue throughout their lives. Qualified, trained teachers teach physical education.

Health Services: Services provided for students to appraise, protect, and promote health. These services are designed to ensure access and referral to primary health care services; foster the appropriate use of primary health care services; prevent and control communicable disease and other health problems; provide emergency care for illness or injury; promote and provide optimal sanitary conditions for a safe school facility and school environment; and provide educational and counseling opportunities for promoting and maintaining individual, family, and community health. Qualified professionals such as physicians, certified school nurses, dentists, health educators, and other allied health personnel provide these services.

Nutrition Services: Access to a variety of nutritious and appealing meals that accommodate the health and nutrition needs of all students. School nutrition programs reflect the federal government's Dietary Guidelines for Americans and other criteria to achieve nutrition integrity. The school nutrition service offers students a learning laboratory for classroom nutrition and health education, and serves as a resource for linkage with nutrition-related community services. Qualified child nutrition professionals provide these services.

Counseling, Psychological, and Social Services: Services provided to improve students' mental, emotional, and social health. These services include individual and group assessments, interventions, and referrals. Organizational assessment and consultation skills of counselors and psychologists contribute not only to the health of students but also to the health of the school environment. Professionals such as certified school counselors, psychologists, and social workers provide these services.

Healthy School Environment: The physical and aesthetic surroundings and the psychological climate and culture of the school. Factors that influence the physical environment include the school building and the area surrounding it; any biological or chemical agents that are detrimental to health; and physical conditions such as temperature, noise, and lighting. The psychological environment includes the physical, emotional, and social conditions that affect the well-being of students and staff.

Health Promotion for Staff: Opportunities for school staff to improve their health status through activities such as health assessments, health education, and health-related fitness activities. These opportunities encourage school staff to pursue a healthy lifestyle that contributes to their improved health status, improved morale, and a greater personal commitment to the school's overall coordinated health program. This personal commitment often transfers into greater commitment to the health of students and creates positive role modeling. Health promotion activities have improved productivity, decreased absenteeism, and reduced health insurance costs.

Parent/Community Involvement: An integrated school, parent, and community approach for enhancing the health and well being of students. School health advisory councils, coalitions, and broadly based constituencies for school health can build support for school health program efforts. Schools actively solicit parent involvement and engage community resources and services to respond more effectively to the health-related needs of students.

Poor health in all its dimensions interferes with a student's ability to learn. Comprehensive health education and physical education aim to assist students to enact health-enhancing behaviors to reduce or eliminate the likelihood of health problems that impede learning and productivity. The Core Curriculum Content Standards for Comprehensive Health Education and Physical Education address the major causes of mortality and morbidity, empowering students to make sound health choices. Comprehensive health education and physical education are two elements of a coordinated school health program designed to foster wellness for students, staff, and community.

Development of Sports and Games

The development of sports and games on a large scale with the object of improving the physical fitness and sportsmanship of the average student as well as of those who excel in this field, has been given its due importance in the National Policy on Education. The Policy has also laid down the need to involve, students in national service through participation in meaningful and challenging programmes of community service.

National Service Scheme

In India, though originally conceived as an alternative to the National Cadet Corps programme to cover every boy student studying in the first degree course of college education, the National Service Scheme was started late in 1969 on a selective and volunteer basis because of the constraint on resources and the need for gaining experience before embarking on a large scale compulsory programme. The Fourth Plan outlay for this programme was fixed at Rs. 5 crores. The per capita cost on this programme estimated at Rs. 150 per year is shared by the Centre and the State in the ratio 2: 1. of the Centre share of Rs. 100/- Rs. 70/ are paid to the State and the balance of Rs. 30/- is to be spent towards grants to selected schools of social work who have been attached to various universities to give orientation training to NSS teachers, to develop the programme and organise All India camps and for grants to the three specialised Institutes namely, The Tata Institute of Social Sciences, Bombay, the Delhi School of Social Work, Delhi and the Indian Institute of Technology, Kharagpur, for research and evaluation, for providing necessary training facilities and for production of literature necessary for the programme. The Centre's share of Rs. 70/- together with the State's share of Rs. 50/- is made available for utilisation by the universities and the colleges in the development of the programme.

The NSS programme launched in September, 1969 in 40 selected educational institution covering 40,000 students has been extended to most universities during subsequent year and the target for 1971-72 was of 1,17,000 students. The programme had its initial teething troubles mainly be, cause the State, Governments could not provide their share of the expenditure in their budget proposals. But this difficulty has 1972- 73 is also 1,60,000 students since been overcome. The targeted strength for the NSS during 1972-73 is also 1,60,000 students.

During the year 1971-72, the social services rendered by the university students covered many aspects like adoption of a village by a university for intensive social uplift work, carrying out of socio- medical surveys, setting up of medical centres, imparting training to rural women in sewing, embroidery and knitting etc. Work in the urban areas ranged from social service to slum dwellers, mass immunization and sanitation drives running of welfare centres, adult education programmes for the poorer sections of the community, blood donation and campaign work in slum areas. Social service, under this scheme was also rendered in the form of help to patients in hospitals, inmates of the orphanages, Cheshire Homes and welfare institutions for the physically handicapped. Work projects were also carried out.

The most important social service rendered during the year was in the Central refugee camps set up for the refugees from Bangla Desh Batches of NSS students from various universities served in these camps for 10 to 15 days at a time by rotation. In all about 15,000 students rendered such service. While proceeding to the refugee camps, the NSS students also collected donation in cash and kind for the refugees.

861 NSS teachers have so far been given orientation training in the 18 selected schools of social work. Training of more NSS teachers for the increased NSS strength for the year 197273 is now contemplated. The three schools of social work have also carried out the evaluation of the NSS programme in a limited number of universities. On the basis of the experience gained during the past two years of NSS activity, a working group is currently examining the modifications necessary to make the programme more realistic and meaningful both from the educational and service angles so as to make the programme more practical and effective.

Another significant feature of national service by students is their involvement in the work of "Chittranjan Mobile Hospitals" established at the rate of one such hospital per State, as part of the C. R. Das centenary celebrations. These hospitals are attached to at least one Medical College in each State. On each mobile hospital the Union Ministry would meet the non-recurring expenditure of Rs. 3 lakhs to meet the cost of capital equipment including the vehicle. Dr. P.K. Doraiswami, Adviser on Mobile Hospitals in the Department of Health in the Ministry of Health and Family Planning is also adviser for the Chittaranjan Mobile Hospital scheme. All the sixteen States to which the scheme was offered have set up these mobile hospitals.

In order to facilitate the setting up of these hospitals as expenditiously as possible, the types of equipment and appliances required were standardised and specifications communicated to the Deans and State authorities concerned. A Blue print for locating tents, the operation theatre, the out-patient department, staff quarters etc., was sent to each Dean.

Detailed guidelines were also supplied to the Deans. A closely coordinated programme of visiting houses in the villages for collecting information regarding the families etc., was worked out in collaboration with the primary health centres and the medical college concerned.

The training and service programme is closely supervised by the teachers from, the medical college in collaboration with the personnel employed in various national programmes. These services include out-patient and in-patient and laboratory work in the mobile hospital, home visiting for health survey and natal clinic, baby welfare motivation in family, planning antemorbidity surveys, collection of vital statistics, involvement in national programmes for eradication or control of communicable diseases, and family planning programme in collaboration with the State Public Health and Family Planning personnel and assistance in the implementation of nutrition, mid-day meal and school health service programmes.

Even within the short time, that the scheme has been in implementation, it has proved to be very popular with the villagers. It has also fulfilled its other main objective of training the students and interns in preventive and promotive aspects of health. The villagers appropriate the health and medical care given by competent specialists near their homes. The scheme has also provided an incentive to those villagers who can afford, to make contributions for starting dispensaries on their own as permanent arrangement after the Mobile Hospital move out, as was evident in the village of Gummidipundi, about 65 kms from Madras. During 1971-72 up to 31st December, 1971 grants totalling Rs, 30,60,000 have been sanctioned to the State Governments. In addition grants of Rs. 20,000 each were sanctioned to four universities for organising the All India NSS camps for the relief of the refugees from Bangla Desh in which over 1800 NSS students have so far participated. So far grants to the extent of Rs.58,412 have been given to the specialised institutions during the year 1971-72.

Youth Welfare Boards and Committees

Under this scheme financial assistance is given to cover 50 per cent of the administrative expenditure incurred by universities on the employment of a wholetime Director or Dean of Students Welfare and a small complement of staff to assist him beside miscellaneous contingent expenditure on certain approved items. At present about 40 universities have set up such boards and committees. A provision of Rs. 0.75 lakhs has been made for the year 1972-73. A proposal is under the consideration of the U. G. C. to merge this Scheme with the other Youth Welfare, Schemes for Universities. Until this materialises, the Ministry of Education, and Social Welfare will continue to operate it.

National Programme for Non-student Youth

On the basis of the recommendations made by the National Advisory Board on Youth, this Ministry had prepared the National Programme for Non-student Youth with an outlay of Rs. 5 crores for the Fourth Plan period after the Cabinet approved in principle an outline of the programme in their meeting dated 1st June, 1970. The following schemes were proposed under the national programme and the financial implications are indicated below:

(Rs; in lakhs)

1.	Establishment of Youth Centres at the District and Block levels	250.00
2.	Development of Play Fields in urban areas	85.00
3	Setting up of Reception Centres in two Metropolitan cities	13.00
4	Development of Camping Sites	40.00
5.	(a) Development of cycling, trekking and hiking routes	70.00
	b) Adventure facilities for cycling, camping, coastal sailing, mountaineering and climbing	

6.	Training Programmes for youth leaders	7.20
7	Work Centres	30.0
8	Miscellaneous	4.80
		500.00

These proposals were considered and approved by the Planning Commission. The Ministry of Finance, while agreeing to the implementation of the schemes relating to development of play-fields and establishment of work-centres, with an outlay of Rs. 115 lakhs during the Fourth Plan suggested that all other schemes be deferred untill the Bangla Desh refugee problems is settled. Orders have already been issued towards implementation of the schemes for the Development of Play Fields and Work Centres with a Provision of Rs. 25 lakhs and Rs. 15 lakhs, respectively during 1971-72.

Under the Scheme of Work Centres, financial assistance of Rs. 1 lakh has already been sanctioned by Government of India to the Calcutta Youth Self-Employment Centre (CYSEC) a voluntary organisation registered under the Indian Societies Registration Act, 1860 (Act 21 of 1860). The CYSEC which is a joint venture sponsored by a representative cross-section of industries, business enterprises, social service organisations and financial institutions have undertaken a number of projects, offering facilities of self- employment to unemployed youth.

Scouting and, Guiding

Financial assistance is given for the promotion of scouting and guilding, which is an international movement. The objective is character building among boys and girls, training them in the art of citizenship and inculcating in them a love of country and a broad- minded approach which will take into account the opinions of others. Financial assistance is made available to the National Headquarters of Bharat Scouts and Guides, New Delhi to meet part of its organisational expenses as well as expenditure on approved items like training camps, national and international Jamborees and participation in international events like camps and rallies.

Scheme of Assistance to Voluntary Organisations in the Field of Youth Services

Assistance is given to voluntary organisations of an all India character for activities engaged in or promoting national integration, Significant experimental or pilot projects, research in youth work, training of personnel for youth work, organisation of conferences, tours, festivals, seminars, refresher courses, workshop devoted to problems of youth welfare, camps and any other services which help in strengthening national cohesion quality for assistance under the scheme.

The grant in aid from the Government of India is given, up to 80 per cent of the non-recurring expenditure subject to a ceiling of Rs. 10,000 per project. If the Government is satisfied that an organisation has already done good work, has competence and ability to continue it, financial assistance may be given to such an orgnisation on three occasions during the period of five years.

National Physical Efficiency Drive

Up to the year 1970-71, the National Physical Efficiency Drive was being organised every year directly by the Ministry of Education & Social Welfare. However, with a view to giving the 'Drive' a fresh impetus in an effort to extend its coverage further, the organisation of the 'Drive' with effect from the year 1971-72 has been entrusted to the Lakshmibai College of Physical Education, Gwalior, which is a national institution in the field of Physical Education fully financed by the Government of India and which possesses the technical know-how that is so necessary for the success of a programme of this kind.

The Ministry of Education and Social Welfare had undertaken to evolve "National Norms" of Physical Fitness for use in the scheme of National Physical Efficiency Drive. The data for evolving these Norms were collected with the assistance of some of the State Liaison Officers connected with the National Physical Efficiency Drive. The task of processing the data towards evolving the "National Norms" was entrusted to the Gokhale Institute of Politics & Economics, Poona. This assignment has now been completed by the Institute. The National Physical Efficiency Drive for 1971-72 was organised in different States & Territories from October, 1971 to January 1972. As against the actual participation of 10.6 lakhs in 1970-71, a participation target of 18.5 lakhs has been suggested for the 1971-72 Drive.

The Tenth All India Competition for the National Award in Physical Efficiency was organised by the Ministry of Education and Social Welfare on the 22nd and 23rd February, 1971, at the, Y.M.C.A. College, of Physical Education, Madras. Out of the 54 competitors who participated in the Competition from various States and Union Territories, 18 competitors-10 men and 8 women-won the National Awards.

Seminars on Physical Education

The Eleventh All-India Seminar on National Physical Efficiency Drive for the States' Representatives and others was held at Gulmarg (J. & K.) from the 1st to 3rd July, 1971. The seminar reviewed the progress of the 1970-71 'Drive' and considered ways and means of accelerating the coverage under the 1971-72 "Drive".

An All-India Seminar for the Principals of Physical Education Teacher Training Institutions was organised by the Ministry of Education and Social Welfare at the Lakshmibai College of Physical Education (Gwalior) from the 14th to 17th October, 1971 the Seminar, which was inaugurated by Shri K. S. Ramaswamy, Union Deputy Minister for Education and Social Welfare, was attended by representatives of 37 training institutions from different parts of the country. The Seminar Considered and adopted with certain modifications the draft curricula of Physical Education, for the various levels of education, including teacher training, prepared earlier by the 'Workshop' organised by the Lakshmibai College of Physical Education, (Gwalior).

Promotion of Yoga

In accordance with the, policy to assist Yoga Institutions of an all-India character for the promotion of research and/or teacher training activities, the Kaivalyadham Shreeman Madhava Yoga Mandira Samiti, Lonavla (Poona) and the Vishwayatan Yogashram (Katra Vaishnavi Devi (J & K) and New Delhi Centres) continued to receive assistance for their recurring as well as non-recurring expenditure.

Promotion of Popular Literature on Physical Education, Games and Sports

The Second National Prize Competition for Published Literature on Physical Education, Sports and Games etc. was organised through the Lakshmibai College of Physical Education (Gwalior). In all, 17 entries were received. As against 5 prizes sanctioned, only one book has been recommended by the Evaluation Committee for a cash prize of Rs. 1,000/- and for purchase by the Government, of 250 copies of the book for free distribution among the Physical Education Training Institutions and other similar institutions.

The Ministry of Education and Social Welfare has undertaken, through the National Institute of Sports, Patiala, publication of introductory booklets on selected games/sports, particularly for the benefit of students. During the year, 4 booklets, on Kabbadi, Tennis, Badminton and Basket Ball, have been brought out.

Improvement of Facilities in Physical Education Training Institutions.

This scheme has replaced the earlier scheme of strengthening Physical Education Training Institutions which was being implemented by the Ministry during the Second and Third Plan Periods. The present scheme will cover both government and non-government institutions in the programme of assistance. The scheme forms part of the overall programme of the Ministry for assistance to the State Sports Councils for development of games and sports. It provides for Central Government's assistance to the physical education training institutions through the State Sports Councils to cover 50 per cent of the expenditure on the following projects subject to the ceiling indicated against each:

Project	*Ceiling of Central Government's Grant*
(i) Gymnasium Hall	Rs 50,000/-
(ii) Development of Play-grounds	Rs. 20,000/-
(iii) Swimming Pool	Rs. 25,000/
(iv) Purchase of Sports equipment & Library Books	Rs. 10,000/-

Society for the National Institutes of Physical Education and Sports (SNIPES)

The Society for the National Institutes of Physical Education & Sports, an autonomous body set up by the Government of India, as the governing body of the two national institutes viz., Lakshmibai College of Physical Education (Gwalior) and National Institute of Sports (Patiala), has been reconstituted for another term of 3 years.

National Fitness Corps

In 1965, the National Fitness Corps Programme was accepted as the only integrated multipurpose programme of Physical education at the school stage, to replace various programmes like Physical Training, National Discipline Scheme and Auxiliary Cadet Corps. In accordance with this decision, the instructors in the National Fitness Corps Organisation, paid out of the Central exchequer, were to be transferred to the States where they were working. As a part of the, terms of such transfer. It was decided in 1969 that the States should be requested to create suitable vacancies in the appropriate department for the absorption of the instructors. It was also decided that the shortfall between the pay and allowances fixed in the State scales of pay and the emoluments last drawn under the Union Government should be treated as personal pay and paid to the instructors for the duration of the fourth Plan period. It was also decided that the Union Government would meet in full the expenditure on pay and allowances of the N.D.C. instructors absorbed by the States for the entire 4th Plan period.

Accordingly, all the State Governments and Union Territory Administrations were required to take over the NDS, Instructors. As a result of the negotiations the Governments of Gujarat, Mysore, Maharashtra, Orissa, Punjab, Himachal Pradesh, Jammu & Kashmir, Delhi, Goa Manipur and Tripura have formally agreed to take over the NDS Instructors. Only U.P., M.P. and Kerala have formally refused. The other States have agreed in principle to take them over but the terms have yet to be communicated by them.

National Sports Organisation

The National Sports Organisation aims at promoting excellence amongst college students in selected fields of Sports and Games. For this purpose, it is necessary to provide better facilities in colleges and universities to encourage sports activities amongst students. The following major programmes were continued during 1971-72.

(i) Development of physical facilities in the universities.

(ii) Provision of coaches.

(iii) Organising coaching camps.

(iv) Award of sports talent scholarships.

The first two programmes are being implemented by the UGC while the last two have been entrusted to the Inter-Univer-sity Sports Board of India and Ceylon. Progress on these programmes is indicated below:

(a) *Physical Facilities:* Out of the Plan outlay of Rs. 1.5 crores for the NSO programme, a sum of Rs. 1,06,50,000/has been earmarked for the improvement of the existing physical facilities and provision of additional facilities in universities/ colleges. Grants totalling Rs. 50.50 lakhs have so far been released to the UGC during 1969-70 and 1970-71. The UGC provides financial assistance to a number of universities/colleges for the construction of gymnasia. In accordance with the recommendations of the Informal Committee on NSO, it has been decided to consider also the, question of giving financial assistance for a number of multipurpose playing fields, each of which would have a pavilion and fields for games like hockey, football, basketball, volleyball, track for the atheletic event and for the improvement of existing swimming pools and for the construction of new swimming pools in selected areas. For this purpose, a standard multipurpose playing fields manual has been prepared in English.

(b) *Coaches:* The UGC provides assistance towards the appointment of NIS-trained coach up to 75 per cent of the expenditure. Out of a total of 100 coaches envisaged in the NSO programme, the UGC has so far agreed to give financial assistance for the employment of 76 coaches.

(c) *Coaching Camps:* While during 1970-71 the IUB held 37 University-Level coaching camps in different games during the year 1971-72, 80 coaching camps are proposed to be held During 1972-73, 24 Zonal Level coaching camps and 110 University Level coaching Camps will be held.

(d) *Sports Talent Scholarship:* The NSO programme inter- alia provides for the award of Sports Talent Scholarships for helping outstanding sportsmen/sports women in their studies as well as in maintaining their physical standards, purchase of equipment, clothing etc. Under the scheme, 50 such scholarships of Rs. 100/- each tenable for 10 months during a year for 2 years, were awarded in 70-71. During 1971-72, 50 fresh scholarships will be awarded.

(e) *Strengthening of Staff for Implementing the NSO Programme:* During the year 1970-71 an amount of Rs. 26,210.17 was granted to the IUB for strengthening the staff and for the year 1971- 72 financial assistance amounting to Rs. 39,000/has been approved.

All India Council of Sports

The National Council of Sports and Physical Education formed on the 10th December, 1970 replaced the All India Council of Sports. On reconsideration it has been decided to revive the All India Council of Sports with more broad based membership giving proper representation in the Council to outstanding sportsmen.

Grants to States Councils

The enlarged and revised scheme of financial assistance to State Sports Council to enable them to construct utility Stadia, to improve the existing Stadia, floodight the stadia, holding annual coaching camps, purchase sports equipment and to establish rural Sports Centres, continued during 1971-72.

Rural Sports Centres

The Scheme of establishment of Rural Sports Centres continued during 1971-72. Central assistance for the establishment of Rural Sports Centres has been given to the States of Maharashtra, Rajasthan, Orissa and Tamil Nadu.

Sports Talent Search Scholarships for School Children

780 Scholarships at Rs. 50/- p.m. on the basis of performance in National Sports Competitions, and 396 scholarships at Rs. 25 p.m. on the basis of performance at State Level Sports Competitions, have been awarded for the year 1971-72 to school students between the age of 14 to 19. 45 National Level scholarships and 69 state level scholarships of the previous year have also been renewed.

Grants to Sports Federations

During the year, grants totalling Rs. 11,56,611 upto 22nd December, 1971 were paid to the National Sports Federations for holding annual championships, participation in international Sports Competitions, visits of foreign teams to India, meeting the salaries of paid Assistant Secretaries, holding Coaching Camps, purchase of Sports equipments and the implementation of Sports items under cultural agreements.

Rural Sports Competition

The Second All India Rural Sports Competition is proposed to be held at Patiala in March 1972 in certain selected games by the N.I.S. Patiala and will be open only to non-student rural youth. About 1000 competitors and officials are expected to participate in this tournament.

National Sports Centre

It has been decided to start, the construction of an Indoor Stadium according to International Specifications and to provide a cycle Track. The scheme is estimated to cost about Rs. 2.53 crores in the Rajghat Sports Complex in New Delhi. This will provide the nucleus of the National Sports Complex for stagging Asian and other international games in course of time.

National Institute of Sports, Patiala

The National Institute of Sports which was established by the Government of India in the year 1961 has made rapid strides in its 10 years of existence. The Institute has so for produced 1767 qualified coaches in various games and sports. During the year 1971-72, 252 persons are under training in the Regular and Condensed Courses. In addition 314 Teachers were oriented in coaching through a 6 week short course run during summer vacations. The number of students admitted for 1971-72 session includes 5 students from Nigeria, 3 from Malaysia, one from Ceylon and one from Nepal. To polish National teams before their participation in International events, 13

Coaching Camps were conducted at the Institute during the year. Under the National Coaching Scheme about 200 NIS paid coaches are working all over the country. Regional Coaching Centres have been established at Delhi, Hyderabad, Jaipur, Lucknow, Nagpur, Bangalore, Gandhi Nagar (Gujarat), Cuttack, Jabalpur, Patna, Jammu/Srinagar and Amritsar.

The National Institute of Sports has now become a premier Sports Institution in Asia. The Institution now functions as the headquarters of the Asian Track and Field Coaches Association, Asian Track and Field Statistical Research Centre, Asian Association of Sports Medicine and Indian Track and Field Coaches Association. During the year 1971 the Institute organised a National Seminar on Sports Medicine and an All-India Conference of State Sports Councils and the First All-India Rural Sports Tournaments.

Coaches from the U.S.A., the U.K. and West Germany visited the Institution for short periods under various Cultural Exchange Programmes for holding clinics for coaches and imparting instruction to trainees. Indian Coaches have also been deputed to countries abroad for advanced studies, where necessary. Under its publication programmes the Institute has published low priced books on Playing-Field Manual Kabbadi, Badminton, Tennis and Basketball The Institute is also bringing out a Quartely NIS Journal containing technical articles on games and sports and Atheletic Asia which is a biannual publication in the field of Athletics.

The Institute is celebrating its 10th Anniversary in March 1972. The Prime Minister visited the Institute and laid the Foundation Stone for a Modern Swimming Pool and Gynasium at the Institute.

Indo-foreign Cultural Exchanges in the Field of Sports in 1971-72

A sports delegation from the USSR consisting of two delegates and one interpreter visited India during April 1971 and met the senior officials of the Ministry and visited the N. I. S.,

Patiala, and the LCPE, Gwalior. The F. R. G. made the services of an athletic coach available to the N.I.S., Patiala for a period of two months in August 1971 to train Indian athletes. An Indian football team visited the USSR for 3 weeks in October-November, 1971 to play friendly matches in that country.

The Indian Mountaineering Foundation

The Indian Mountaineering Foundation, an autonomous organisation to promote mountaineering, rock climbing as well as other adventure programmes received grants in aid from the Ministry. The Foundation given financial assistance for approved mountaineering expectations. Grants in aid amounting Rs. 1 lakh have been released to the Foundation for the month ended December, 1971.

National Integration-Inter State Students-Teacher Camps on "Out India Project".

The main objective of the camps under the scheme is to provide opportunities for the change of visits by groups of students from one part of the country to another so that they may learn about their rich cultural heritage and history, discover their common bonds and the underlying theme of National Unity amidst the cultural pluralism and diversity of India financial assistance has been given to the National council of Educational Research and Training and the Kendriya Vidyalaya.

Sangathan to organise camps under this scheme of 10 to 15 days duration in which participants from schools and 4 or different States stay in a school in a sixth State Under "Our India Project", 100 selected schools are helped to collect information from schools and organise the "Our India Exhibition" to be shown around neighbouring schools. These projects envisage an expenditure of 50 lakhs during the Fourth Plan period.

3

Scope of Physical Education

Healthy active living involves a combination of physical activity and appropriate lifestyle choices. Students should begin early on to acquire basic knowledge about a wide variety of health-related topics and to develop relevant skills. They need to understand how their actions and decisions affect their health, fitness, and personal well-being, and how to apply their learning to make positive, healthy decisions in all areas of life and personal development. The school environment can profoundly influence students' attitudes, preferences, and behaviours.

Through the health and physical education curriculum, students will develop:

— an understanding of the importance of physical fitness, health, and well-being and the factors that contribute to them;

— a personal commitment to daily vigorous physical activity and positive health behaviours;

— the basic movement skills they require to participate in physical activities throughout their lives.

The achievement of the objectives of the health and physical education program will not only enhance each student's life but will also result in a healthier population. Students' knowledge of the importance of daily vigorous physical activity will also help them understand how such activity combats health risks such as obesity and heart disease.

A comprehensive approach to health and physical education emphasizes the shared responsibility of parents, peers, schools, health-care systems, government, the media, and a variety of other institutions and agencies. Meaningful health and physical education also requires safe, health-promoting environments, support services from the community, and a school curriculum that makes health a priority in the school.

The Role of Parents

Studies show that students perform better in school if their parents are involved in their education. Parents therefore have an important role to play in supporting their children's learning. By reading the curriculum, parents can find out what their children are learning in each grade and why they are learning it. This knowledge of the curriculum will enable parents to discuss their children's work with them, to communicate with teachers, and to ask relevant questions about their children's progress. Their knowledge of the expectations in each grade will also help parents interpret their children's report cards and work with teachers to improve students' learning. For this reason, parents are urged to read the expectations for all grades rather than just the particular grades their children are in.

Parents can also participate in parent conferences, work on school councils, and become involved in physical activities with their children. They should support classroom activities, promote and participate both in special events held within the school and in interschool activities, and promote healthy active living through their own habits and practices. They should also support healthy eating and take responsibility for developing their children's self-esteem.

The Role of Teachers

Teachers and students have complementary responsibilities. Teachers are responsible for developing a variety of appropriate instructional strategies that will involve students actively in the curriculum and at the same time address different student needs. They should bring enthusiasm to the classroom and should model healthy active living in their own lives to encourage students to recognize the value and relevance of what they are learning.

The Role of Students

Students have responsibilities with regard to their own learning, which increase as they advance through elementary and secondary school. Those willing to make the effort required and able to apply themselves soon learn that there is a direct relationship between achievement and hard work. Such students become motivated, self-directed learners. Some students, however, find it more difficult to take responsibility for their learning because of special challenges they face. For these students, the attention, patience, and encouragement of teachers can be extremely important factors for success. Regardless of their circumstances, learning to take responsibility for their own progress and learning is an important part of education for all students.

Health and Physical Education Curriculum

The curriculum's major areas of knowledge and skills are organized around three strands:

— Healthy living includes healthy eating, growth and development, personal safety and injury prevention, and substance use and abuse.

— Fundamental movement skills include locomotion/travelling, manipulation, and stability.

— Active participation includes physical activity, physical fitness, living skills, and safety.

These strands combine the living skills (e.g., personal, interpersonal, communication, conflict-resolution, goal-setting, organizational, time-management, problem-solving, and decision-making skills) that all students require.

Schools must develop procedures to ensure the highest possible level of safety, while allowing students to engage in a broad range of challenging activities. Safety guidelines should outline the practices to be followed for each activity, addressing questions related to equipment, clothing, facilities, special rules and instructions, and supervision. They should also reflect school board policies on how to conduct activities, and they should be reviewed on a regular basis. While all physical activity involves an element of risk, participants have an obligation to minimize that risk. Concern for safety should be an integral part of curriculum planning and implementation.

The primary responsibility for ensuring safe practices rests with the school district and its employees. Wherever possible, potential risks must be identified and procedures developed to prevent or minimize accidents or injuries. In a safe classroom, the teacher will be aware of up-to-date safety information, will observe students carefully, show foresight, and act quickly. By implementing safe instructional practices (e.g., logical teaching progressions and age- appropriate activities), educators can reduce risks and guard against accidents. In a safe school, students will:

— follow established routines for physical activities (e.g., set procedures for entering and leaving the gym and changing clothes, warm-up and cool-down activities);

— wear clothing appropriate to activities (e.g., a hat for outdoor activities), wear appropriate footwear and ensure that shoelaces are tied, and remove jewellery when participating in physical activities;

— follow the instructions outlined for each activity (e.g., for starting and stopping);

— take age-appropriate responsibility (e.g., for the safe use of equipment) and necessary precautions (e.g., use a safety mat);

— follow rules and expectations pertaining to the setting for the activity (e.g., ski only in designated areas, follow playground rules);

— recognize and report unsafe situations and conditions;

— always play safely.

Student's Attitudes

Students' attitudes towards health and physical education can have a significant effect on their achievement of the expectations. To learn effectively and develop positive attitudes towards healthy active living, students should enjoy the skill-development and physical activities. They should also come to recognize the importance of observing safety procedures, respecting others, and being punctual.

The curriculum provides students with opportunities to use software programs, the Internet, e-mail, and audio and visual technology for a variety of purposes. For example, students can use technology to record food choices over a period of time, measure nutrient intake, maintain a fitness profile, evaluate an individual's physical stages, monitor physical performance, and develop personal exercise programs. They can use the World Wide Web to access and research information on various health-and-fitness topics and issues.

Planning Student Programs

Teachers must provide a balanced program with a broad selection of activities. In doing so, they can combine expectations from more than one of the three strands to help students see the connections between physical skills and health concepts (e.g., that daily physical activity improves health and physical fitness). Teachers must also ensure that the concepts and skills taught are appropriate to students' ages and stages of development, and to their perceptions, prior knowledge, attitudes, learning styles, and exceptionalities. They must use a variety of instructional approaches to ensure that all students are given every opportunity to learn and perform to their full potential.

This curriculum requires that students participate in vigorous physical activity for a sustained period of time each day. The amount of time suggested is described in the expectations and varies from Grade 1 to Grade 8 in US. This expectation can also be achieved in a variety of ways, using school and community indoor and outdoor facilities. Co-curricular programs. Where possible, the health and physical education curriculum will include both curricular and complementary cocurricular components. Intramural programs allow all students to participate in either same-sex or coeducational activities that are informal and not highly competitive. Interschool programs offer students opportunities to participate in more organized and competitive activities.

Other recreational activities and clubs also provide opportunities for students with common interests and a desire to participate in physical activities in non-competitive settings. In planning and organizing the health and physical education curriculum, schools should use community organizations, facilities, and programs as resources to provide students with additional experiences and opportunities for physical activities. Coeducational and segregated classes.

Although all the curriculum expectations can be achieved in either coeducational or same-sex classes, some expectations can be addressed more effectively in same-sex settings. For example, discussions involving topics of a sensitive nature, especially those in the Healthy Living strand, can be uncomfortable for some students, but these same students might feel quite secure and comfortable discussing these topics in a same-sex setting. Similarly, when expectations related to skill development (particularly team-sport skills) are addressed, same-sex classes and groupings might encourage more students to become physically active and to participate in the interschool program, as well as in community activities. Teachers should base their decisions as to whether to teach in coeducational or segregated settings on the sensitivity of topics and students' needs.

Planning for the coeducational classroom

Acknowledgement of and respect for individual differences will encourage student participation and help students learn to collaborate with and respect others. They will also enhance students' competence, self-esteem, health, and well-being. The health and physical education program will address students' awareness of and esteem for each other. Strategies for encouraging this awareness and mutual respect among students include:

— providing opportunities for both male and female students to assume leadership roles;

— encouraging and respecting the interests and abilities of both genders;

— ensuring that responsibilities are shared equally by male and female students;

— expecting all students to be equally active participants;

— creating a class atmosphere that helps students develop consideration for, understanding of, and respect for each other.

Cross-curricular planning

Health and physical education are essential to the entire school curriculum. Studies show that students who participate in physical activity each day exhibit improved memory, concentration, and communication, problem-solving, and leadership abilities, which improve their learning in other subject areas. Such students also display more positive attitudes towards themselves, improved interpersonal behaviour, and a willingness to meet and deal with the challenges of daily life. Because active learning is so important for all students, daily vigorous physical activity in elementary schools is strongly encouraged by the provincial curriculum. The development of skills and knowledge in the areas of health and physical education is related to learning in other subjects.

When planning programs, teachers should emphasize such cross-curricular relationships by co-ordinating the teaching of related expectations. For example, in Grade 5, students could describe the short- and long-term effects of alcohol (health and physical education), learn about its properties (science and technology), and represent in a graph the results of a survey of a select group of people with regard to its use and abuse (mathematics). At the conclusion of the unit, students could be asked to report orally or in writing (language arts) on the impact of alcohol on people's lives.

Health and Physical Education for Exceptional Students

Recognizing the needs of exceptional students and providing appropriate programs and services for them are important aspects of planning and implementing the curriculum. Specific procedures are set out in legislation for the identification and placement of exceptional students. The needs of exceptional students are identified by an Identification, Placement, and Review Committee (IPRC). When an IPRC identifies a student as exceptional, an Individual Education Plan (IEP) must be developed and maintained for that student. (It should be noted that an IEP may also be prepared for students with special needs who are receiving special education programs and/or services but who have not been identified as exceptional by an IPRC).

An IEP defines the student's educational program as one that is based on and modified by the results of continuous assessment and evaluation. It identifies the student's specific learning expectations and explains how the school will address these expectations (for example, through appropriate programs and services, modifications in the regular program, and other accommodations). It also identifies the methods by which the student's progress will be reviewed.

In developing the student's IEP, consideration must be given to any recommendations made by the IPRC concerning programs and services that may be particularly appropriate for meeting the student's needs. Also, the school must consult with the parents of the student at the development stage. The IPRC's recommendations and the results of consultation between the parents and the school staff will form the basis of decisions concerning the ways in which the learning expectations set out in the provincial curriculum will be modified to meet the student's special needs.

Once the IEP has been developed, the parents of the student must be provided with a copy. Those involved in developing the IEP should work together on an ongoing basis to review the student's progress and make adjustments to the IEP as necessary. It is important that the school continue to keep parents informed about the program and the progress of the student, as parents can provide valuable support for their child's learning. In health and physical education, exceptional students may need a variety of modifications both to the program itself and to the learning environment. These modifications may include:

- facilities that allow for the mobility of students with physical disabilities;
- equipment modifications that enable all students to perform to their full potential (e.g., increasing the length of a scoop handle to enable a student who uses a wheelchair to reach the floor);
- program modifications (e.g., altering the method of instruction);
- assessment and evaluation strategies that accommodate a variety of learning styles and needs;

— encouraging as much student participation as possible in planning, instruction, assessment, and evaluation;
— using support systems extensively.

Since equipment and facilities in individual schools will vary across the province, care has been taken in this curriculum to ensure that students can meet the expectations in a variety of settings and with a broad range of equipment. The curriculum stresses daily active participation in physical activities that do not necessarily require the use of a school gymnasium. Teachers are encouraged to use various school and community facilities for their programs – schoolyards, soccer fields, baseball diamonds, football fields, swimming pools, arenas – and to help students develop specific skills through a variety of activities. Exposure to these various settings will increase students' awareness of community facilities.

Teachers can use equipment to focus on students' specific skill development and to vary physical activities. When supplies are limited, teachers will have to be resourceful to ensure that each student has opportunities to use various types of equipment. For example, an activity that focuses on catching objects of various sizes and shapes could include the use of bean bags, tennis balls, beach balls, and Frisbees. Teachers must provide specific instruction to students on the appropriate handling of equipment, ensure that equipment is in good repair and suitably organized, and take into account the height, weight, and ages of the students using the equipment.

Curriculum Expectations and Levels of Achievements

There are four categories of skills in health and physical education: understanding of concepts, movement skills, active participation, and communication of required knowledge. For each of these categories, there are four levels of achievement. These levels are brief descriptions of degrees of achievement that teachers will use as the basis for their assessment of each student's work.

Teachers should use the descriptions to identify the level at which a student has achieved a particular expectation, or a group of expectations, in the appropriate category of knowledge or skills. For example, they could use it as a guide when observing students' performance or to explain the different levels of achievement to parents.

Understanding of concepts

The student:

— shows understanding of few of the required concepts taught with major errors or omissions;

— shows understanding of some of the required concepts taught with several minor errors or omissions;

— shows understanding of most of the required concepts taught with a few minor errors or omissions;

— shows understanding of all or almost all of the required concepts taught with practically no errors or omissions;

Movement skills (locomotion/travelling, manipulation, and stability)

The student:

— performs few of the required skills as described

— rarely applies the required skills in other situations or activities;

— performs some of the required skills as described;

— sometimes applies the required skills in other situations or activities;

— performs most of the required skills as described;

— usually applies the required skills in other situations or activities;

— performs all or almost all of the required skills as described;

— consistently applies the required skills in other situations or activities;

Active participation

The student:

— participates actively only with constant encouragement;

— applies few of the required skills;

— requires constant reminders regarding safety procedures and the safe use of equipment and facilities;

— participates actively, needing only occasional encouragement;

— applies some of the required skills;

— requires occasional reminders regarding safety procedures and the safe use of equipment and facilities;

— requires no encouragement to participate actively;

— applies most of the required skills;

— follows safety procedures and uses equipment and facilities safely;

— participates actively in a manner that encourages others to participate;

— applies all or almost all of the required skills;

— follows safety procedures and uses equipment and facilities safely, and encourages others to do so;

Communication of required knowledge

The student:

— communicates poorly, making many errors or omissions;

— rarely uses appropriate terminology.

— communicates with some clarity, making some errors or omissions;

— sometimes uses appropriate terminology.

— communicates clearly and precisely, making few errors or omissions;

— usually uses appropriate terminology.

— communicates clearly and precisely, making no or almost no errors or omissions;

— uses appropriate and varied terminology.

Healthy Living Standard

The healthy living strand will provide students with the knowledge and skills they need to develop, maintain, and enjoy healthy lifestyles, as well as to solve problems, make decisions, and set goals that are directly related to personal health and well-being. The four components of this strand are healthy eating, growth and development, personal safety and injury prevention, and substance use and abuse.

Healthy eating

Topics related to healthy eating include nutrition, eating disorders, body image, and dental health. Students require knowledge to make healthy eating choices. Using this knowledge, they will examine their own food choices and eating patterns, and then make wise decisions and set appropriate goals. In later grades, students will learn more about the factors that affect healthy body weight and lead to eating disorders, and will increase their understanding of a healthy body image. Throughout the healthy living strand, the importance of healthy eating and regular physical activity is emphasized.

Growth and development

Growth and development education is more than simply

teaching young people about the anatomy and physiology of reproduction. For example, growth and development education focuses on an understanding of sexuality in its broadest context – sexual development, reproductive health, interpersonal relationships, affection, abstinence, body image, and gender roles. Acquiring information and skills and developing attitudes, beliefs, and values related to identity and relationships are lifelong processes.

Parents and guardians are the primary educators of their children. As children grow and develop relationships with family members and others, they learn about appropriate behaviours and values, as well as about sexuality. They are influenced by parents, friends, relatives, religious leaders, teachers, and neighbours, as well as by television, radio, videos, movies, books, advertisements, music, and newspapers. School-based programs add another important dimension to a child's ongoing learning about sexuality.

The overall and specific expectations in this strand are age-appropriate and should be addressed with sensitivity and respect for individual differences. Because of the sensitive nature of these topics, parents or guardians must be informed about the content of the curriculum and time of delivery. Teachers and learners must develop a comfort level with these topics so that information can be discussed openly, honestly, and in an atmosphere of mutual respect. The "healthy sexuality" expectations should be addressed only after teachers have developed rapport with their students. Opportunities should be provided for segregated as well as coeducational instruction.

Personal safety and injury prevention

Personal safety and injury prevention are essential components of the healthy living strand. Education in these areas is critical for reducing children's injuries. Personal safety topics include bullying, peer assault, child abuse, harassment, and violence in relationships. Injury prevention topics include bicycle safety, seasonal safety rules, sun protection, home safety, fire safety, seat belt use, and first aid. The expectations address the knowledge and skills needed to reduce safety risks at home, at school, and in the community. Students will become familiar with the support available to them within the family as well as with the agencies and services that provide support and help within the community. However, knowledge alone is not enough; students require the necessary skills to respond appropriately to situations that threaten their personal safety and well-being. Living skills such as conflict resolution, assertiveness, resistance and refusal techniques, and decision making will help them respond to situations effectively.

Substance use and abuse

Education is critical to the prevention of drug abuse. Parents, guardians, educators, and society in general all have key roles to play in educating students about drug use and abuse. Alcohol and tobacco are the drugs most readily available to Ontario students, and smoking is the primary cause of preventable illnesses, disabilities, and premature deaths in Canada. The substance use and abuse learning expectations respond to these facts by focusing on an understanding of the effects of drugs – prescription drugs, non-prescription drugs, illicit drugs, tobacco, alcohol – and the consequences of their use. This knowledge is integrated with the development of a variety of living skills that help students make and maintain healthy choices. By using problem-solving, decision-making, refusal, and assertiveness skills effectively, learners can select healthy, drug-free behaviours based on accurate information.

For healthy eating of grade 1 students will:

— identify the food groups and give examples of foods in each group;

— suggest occasions (e.g., a bake sale, a class party) when they can choose healthy food snacks, and describe the factors affecting their choices (e.g., choices made because of allergies or culture);

— describe ways to care for their teeth; for growth and development:

— describe simple life cycles of plants and animals, including humans;

— recognize that rest, food, and exercise affect growth;

— identify the major parts of the body by their proper names;

For personal safety and injury prevention:

— outline the potential safety risks in the home, school, and community (e.g., from fire or toys);

— describe exploitative behaviours (e.g., abusive behaviours, bullying, inappropriate touching) and the feelings associated with them;

— identify people who can provide personal safety assistance (e.g., block parents) and explain how to access them.

For substance use and abuse:

— recognize that there are some medicines (e.g., cough syrup, nose drops) and other substances (e.g., vitamins) that help the body when used properly (safely);

— identify (e.g., from their symbols and labels) medicines and household products that are harmful to the body;

— employ decision-making skills to identify when and how medicines should be used (e.g., seeking out adult assistance).

By the end of Grade 2, students will:

— identify healthy eating practices and use a decision-making model to make healthy food choices;

— describe parts of the human body, the functions of these parts, and behaviours that contribute to good health;

— outline safety rules and safe practices;

— describe the effects on the body of appropriate and inappropriate uses of medicines.

Healthy eating for grade 2 students:

— identify a balanced diet and apply decision-making skills to create menus for healthy meals;

— describe the importance of food to the body (e.g., for energy and growth);

— explain the negative effects of poor nutrition on healthy teeth and the importance of regular brushing and visits to the dentist;

Personal safety and injury prevention:

— identify safety rules to be followed in the home, school, and community (e.g., electrical safety, schoolyard rules, bus safety);

— describe types of verbal and physical violence (e.g., name calling, kicking, hitting);

— explain the importance of being able to say no to exploitative behaviours (e.g., improper touching), and describe how to seek help;

Substance use and abuse:

— describe the difference between prescription and non-prescription medicines;

— outline the safe use of medicines (e.g., the need for an adult to supervise the administration of medicines, taking proper dosages);

— use decision-making skills to identify healthy alternatives to drug use (e.g., fresh air and exercise can help relieve headaches).

By the end of Grade 3, students will:

- describe the relationship among healthy eating practices, healthy active living, and healthy bodies;
- outline characteristics in the development and growth of humans from birth to childhood;
- list safety procedures and practices in the home, school, and community;
- describe what a drug is, list several examples (e.g., nicotine, caffeine, alcohol), and describe the effects of these substances on the body.

For healthy eating:

- identify foods from different cultures and classify them by food groups;
- describe the benefits of healthy food choices, physical activity, and healthy bodies;
- describe a variety of ways to prevent tooth decay (e.g., brushing, making appropriate food choices, rinsing the mouth).

Growth and Development:

- outline the basic human and animal reproductive processes (e.g., the union of egg and sperm);
- describe basic changes in growth and development from birth to childhood (e.g., changes to teeth, hair, feet, and height).

Personal Safety and injury prevention:

- explain relevant safety procedures (e.g., fire drills, railway-crossing and crosswalk procedures);
- use a problem-solving process to identify ways of obtaining support for personal safety in the home, school, and community;

— identify examples of real and fictional violence (e.g., schoolyard fights, cartoons, movies);

Substance use and abuse:

— define the term drug and identify a variety of legal and illegal drugs;

— identify nicotine (in cigarettes), caffeine (in coffee and colas), and alcohol as drugs;

— use decision-making skills to make healthy choices about drug use, and recognize the effects of various substances (e.g., nicotine, caffeine, alcohol) on the body.

By the end of Grade 4, students will:

— explain the role of healthy eating practices, physical activity, and heredity as they relate to body shape and size;

— identify the physical, interpersonal, and emotional aspects of healthy human beings;

— use living skills to address personal safety and injury prevention;

— identify the influences (e.g., the media, peers, family members) affecting the use of tobacco, as well as the effects and legalities of, and healthy alternatives to, tobacco use.

Healthy eating:

— outline the factors that influence body shape and size (e.g., heredity, diet, exercise);

— analyse, over a period of time, their own food selections, including food purchases (e.g., "everyday food" versus "sometimes food") and determine whether or not they are healthy choices;

Growth and development:

— describe the four stages of human development (infancy, childhood, adolescence, and adulthood) and identify the physical, interpersonal, and emotional changes appropriate to their current stage;

— identify the characteristics of healthy relationships (e.g., showing consideration of others' feelings by avoiding negative communication);

— identify the challenges (e.g., conflicting opinions) and responsibilities in their relationships with family and friends;

Personal safety and injury prevention:

— apply decision-making and problem-solving skills in addressing threats to personal safety (e.g., from abuse or physical fighting) and injury prevention (e.g., bicycle safety, road safety);

— identify people (e.g., parents, guardians, neighbours, teachers) and community agencies (e.g., Kids' Help Phone) that can assist with injury prevention, emergency situations, and violence prevention;

Substance use and abuse:

— identify the major harmful substances found in tobacco and explain the term addiction;

— describe the short- and long-term effects of first- and second-hand smoke, and identify the advantages of being smoke-free;

— apply decision-making and assertiveness skills to make and maintain healthy choices related to tobacco use, and recognize factors that can influence decisions to smoke or to abstain from smoking (e.g., the media, family members, friends, laws).

By the end of Grade 5, students will:

- analyse information that has an impact on healthy eating practices (e.g., food labels, food guides, care-of-teeth brochures);
- describe physical, emotional, and interpersonal changes associated with puberty;
- apply strategies to deal with threats to personal safety (e.g., in response to harassment) and to prevent injury (e.g., from physical assault);
- identify the influences (e.g., the media, peers, family) affecting alcohol use, as well as the effects and legalities of, and healthy alternatives to, alcohol use.

Healthy eating

- explain the purpose and function of calories and the major food nutrients;
- identify critical content information on food labels (e.g., ingredients, calories, additives, fat content);
- describe the influence of the media on body image (e.g., shape and size);
- explain how changes in our bodies sometimes affect our eating habits (e.g., increased appetite during growth spurts).

Growth and development:

- identify strategies to deal positively with stress and pressures that result from relationships with family and friends;
- identify factors (e.g., trust, honesty, caring) that enhance healthy relationships with friends, family, and peers;
- describe the secondary physical changes at puberty (e.g., growth of body hair, changes in body shape);

— describe the processes of menstruation and spermatogenesis;

— describe the increasing importance of personal hygiene following puberty.

Personal safety and injury prevention:

— explain how people's actions (e.g., bullying, excluding others) can affect the feelings and reactions of others;

— apply strategies (e.g., anger management, assertiveness, conflict resolution) to deal with personal-safety and injury-prevention situations (e.g., swarming, threatening, harassment).

Substance use and abuse:

— describe the short- and long-term effects of alcohol use and abuse;

— apply decision-making skills to make healthy choices about alcohol use, and recognize factors (e.g., the media, family members, friends, laws) that can influence the decision to drink alcohol;

— demonstrate resistance techniques (e.g., avoidance, walking away) and assertiveness skills (e.g., saying no) to deal with peer pressure in situations pertaining to substance use and abuse.

By the end of Grade 6, students will:

— explain how body image and self-esteem influence eating practices;

— identify the major parts of the reproductive system and their functions and relate them to puberty;

— use basic prevention and treatment skills (e.g., basic first aid) to help themselves and others;

— identify the influences (e.g., the media, peers, family) affecting the use of cannabis and other drugs, as well as the effects and legalities of, as well as healthy alternatives to, cannabis and other drugs.

Healthy eating:

— determine the influence of various factors (e.g., the media, family traditions, allergies) on personal food choices, body image, and self-esteem;

— analyse personal eating habits in a variety of situations (e.g., at home, in school, in restaurants);

— describe the benefits of healthy eating for active living;

Growth and development:

— relate the changes at puberty to the reproductive organs and their functions;

— apply a problem-solving/decision-making process to address issues related to friends, peers, and family relationships;

Personal safety and injury prevention:

— identify and describe appropriate methods for preventing and treating ailments (e.g., sunburn, minor cuts);

— identify the responsibilities associated with caring for themselves and others (e.g., while babysitting);

— describe and respond appropriately to potentially violent situations relevant to themselves (e.g., threats, harassment, violence in the media);

Substance Use and Abuse

— describe the short- and long-term effects of cannabis and other illicit drugs;

— determine influences (e.g., interpersonal, personal, legal, economic) on the use and abuse of tobacco and other drugs (e.g., alcohol, cannabis, LSD) and consider them as part of a decision-making process to make healthy choices;

— identify people and community agencies that support making healthy choices regarding substance use and abuse.

By the end of Grade 7, students will:

— relate healthy eating practices and active living to body image and self-esteem;

— describe age-appropriate matters related to sexuality (e.g., the need to develop good interpersonal skills, such as the ability to communicate effectively with the opposite sex);

— explain how harassment relates to personal safety;

— apply living skills to deal with peer pressure related to substance use and abuse.

Healthy eating:

— examine the effects of healthy eating and regular physical activity on body size and shape, and on self-esteem;

— describe how our body image influences our food choices;

— identify factors affecting healthy body weight (e.g., food intake, growth spurts, physical activity/inactivity);

Growth and development:

— explain the male and female reproductive systems as they relate to fertilization;

— distinguish between the facts and myths associated with menstruation, spermatogenesis, and fertilization;

— identify the methods of transmission and the symptoms of sexually transmitted diseases (STDs), and ways to prevent them;

— use effective communication skills (e.g., refusal skills, active listening) to deal with various relationships and situations;

— explain the term abstinence as it applies to healthy sexuality;

— identify sources of support with regard to issues related to healthy sexuality (e.g., parents/guardians, doctors);

Personal safety and injury prevention:

— describe harassment and identify ways of dealing with it (e.g., by communicating feelings and reporting incidents of harassment);

— identify people and resources that can support someone experiencing harassment;

Substance use and abuse:

— outline a variety of issues related to substance use and abuse (e.g., the effects of second-hand smoke; the impact of laws governing drug use, including the use of tobacco and alcohol);

— identify and categorize drugs as stimulants, depressants, and hallucinogens;

— apply a decision-making process to make informed choices regarding drug use;

— demonstrate strategies (e.g., saying no, walking away) that can be used to counter pressures to smoke, drink, and take drugs, and identify healthy alternatives to drug use.

By the end of Grade 8, students will:

— adopt personal goals that reflect healthy eating practices;

— identify the physical, emotional, interpersonal, and spiritual aspects of healthy sexuality (e.g., respect for life, ethical questions in relationships, contraception);

— identify local support groups and community organizations (e.g., public health offices) that provide information or services related to health and well-being;

— analyse situations that are potentially dangerous to personal safety (e.g., gang violence) and determine how to seek assistance;

— apply living skills (e.g., decision-making, problem-solving, and refusal skills) to respond to matters related to sexuality, drug use, and healthy eating habits.

Healthy eating:

— analyse the effects of undereating (e.g., as a result of bulimia or sports dieting) and overeating (e.g., obesity) on health and well-being;

— identify ways to maintain a healthy body weight (e.g., physical activity);

— adopt personal food plans, based on nutritional needs and personal goals, to improve or maintain their eating practices.

Growth and development:

— explain the importance of abstinence as a positive choice for adolescents;

— identify symptoms, methods of transmission, prevention, and high-risk behaviours related to common STDs, HIV, and AIDS;

— identify methods used to prevent pregnancy;

— apply living skills (e.g., decision-making, assertiveness, and refusal skills) in making informed decisions, and analyse the consequences of engaging in sexual activities and using drugs;

— identify sources of support (e.g., parents/ guardians, doctors) related to healthy sexuality issues;

Personal safety and injury prevention:

— analyse situations (e.g., hitchhiking, gang violence, violence in relationships) that are potentially dangerous to personal safety;

— identify support services (e.g., the school guidance department, shelters, Kids' Help Phone) that assist victims of violence, and explain how to access them;

Substance Use and Abuse

– outline the possible negative consequences of substance use and abuse (e.g., fetal alcohol syndrome, effects of steroid use, accidents when drinking and driving);

— identify those school and community resources that are involved in education about substance use and abuse, and those involved in preventing and treating substance abuse;

— describe causes and symptoms of stress and positive ways (as opposed to substance use) to relieve stress;

— apply the steps of a decision-making process to address age-specific situations related to personal health and well-being in which substance use or abuse is one of the factors.

Basicn Movement Skills

The movement skills are organized into three categories:

— locomotion/travelling, in which the body moves from one point to another (e.g., walking, running, skipping, hopping, galloping, chasing, fleeing, dodging)

— manipulation, which involves giving force to objects or receiving force from objects (e.g., throwing, catching, collecting, kicking, punting, dribbling, volleying, striking)

— stability, in which the body remains in place but moves around its horizontal or vertical axis (e.g., bending, stretching, twisting, turning, rolling, balancing, transferring weight, curling up, landing from a jump)

These basic movement skills are the foundation of all physical activity and are essential both to an individual's development of effective motor skills and to the application of these skills in a wide variety of physical activities. Since the skills can also enhance students' interpersonal, cognitive, and emotional development, it is critical that the health and physical education program be inclusive, engaging all students irrespective of their gender, background, or ability.

When fun and enjoyment are part of skill development and physical activity, students are more likely to develop positive attitudes towards healthy active living.

Students will develop skills related to the following four principles of movement:

— body awareness (what parts the body moves)

— space awareness (where the body moves, e.g., location, direction, or level)

— effort (how the body moves, e.g., fast or slow, with strong or light force, or bound or free)

— relationship (with whom or with what the body moves, e.g., with people or with objects)

Movement principles and skills must be taught in association with other activities. They must also be taught in the proper progression and through age-appropriate activities.

Research into motor development indicates that learners acquire new fundamental movement skills (motor skills) most successfully during the preschool and elementary years as students' neurological pathways are developing rapidly during this period and are receptive to the development of fundamental movement patterns and basic skills. When young children enter school, their movements are often awkward and lacking in fluidity. In the early school years, they gain necessary co-ordination and control over their movements.

They can then refine, extend, and apply these patterns to more complex skills during later childhood, adolescence, and adulthood. For example, the basic skill of throwing an object overhand can be transferred to a tennis serve or badminton smash.

Movement skills must be taught; they are not acquired simply through activities of various sorts. As well, mature movement skills do not result from physical maturation alone; rather, they must be continually refined and combined with other movement skills in a variety of physical activities. Safety must be an integral part of the health and physical education program. While teachers have the ultimate responsibility for matters related to supervision, equipment, facilities, and procedures, students must take some responsibility for their own safety, beginning at a very young age. Following procedures, using equipment as instructed, and wearing appropriate attire are some ways in which students can contribute to their safe participation in physical activity. Safety is addressed in the overall expectations for each grade and is implicit in all of the specific expectations. Students must fulfil each expectation safely and responsibly without putting themselves and others at risk.

Fundamental Movement Skills: Grade 1

By the end of Grade 1, students will:

— perform the basic movement skills required to participate in physical activities: locomotion/travelling (e.g., galloping, running), manipulation (e.g., throwing, catching), and stability (e.g., jumping, landing);

— demonstrate the principles of movement (e.g., in various directions, alone, with others, at various speeds) using locomotion/travelling, manipulation, and stability skills.

Locomotion/Travelling Skills:

— travel in a variety of ways (e.g., leap, gallop) in different directions in response to signals (e.g., stop or go signals);

— travel in a variety of ways using different pathways (e.g., straight, curved, or zigzag pathways in creative dance);

Manipulation Skills:

— throw objects of various sizes and shapes underhand, using one or two hands and large targets (e.g., toss a bean bag through a hoop);

— catch objects of various sizes, shapes, and textures below the waist and using two hands (e.g., catch a utility or beach ball);

— bounce, while stationary, a ball with one hand;

Stability Skills:

— jump forward with control, using a variety of take-offs and landings;

— demonstrate basic static balances (e.g., stork balance) without equipment;

— transfer their weight from one body part to another.

Fundamental Movement Skills: Grade 2

By the end of Grade 2, students will:

— perform the basic movement skills required to participate in physical activities: locomotion/travelling (e.g., skipping, hopping), manipulation (e.g., throwing, bouncing), and stability (e.g., balancing, twisting);

— demonstrate the principles of movement (e.g., at various levels, in relationship to equipment, using different body parts) using locomotion/travelling, manipulation, and stability skills.

Locomotion/Travelling Skills:

— travel and change from one kind of locomotion/ travelling movement to another (e.g., hopping to skipping);

— travel in a variety of ways, changing pathways and directions (e.g., in creative dance, dances from other countries);

Manipulation Skills:

— kick a stationary ball, using either foot, to a partner or to a large target;

— dribble a ball over a short distance, using their feet;

— bounce a ball while moving, using either hand;

Stability Skills:

— jump and land safely, using take-off combinations of one or two feet;

— balance on a variety of body parts, on and off equipment, while stationary and moving (e.g., balancing on a bench without moving, walking forward on a bench);

— transfer their body weight over low equipment in a variety of ways (e.g., from feet to hands to feet).

Fundamental Movement Skills: Grade 3

By the end of Grade 3, students will:

— perform the basic movement skills required to participate in physical activities: locomotion/travelling (e.g., dodging, chasing), manipulation (e.g., striking, hitting), and stability (e.g., balancing on equipment, performing rolls);

— demonstrate the principles of movement (e.g., in various body shapes; using sudden, sustained, fast, or slow movements) using locomotion/travelling, manipulation, and stability skills.

Locomotion/Travelling Skills:

— combine various locomotion/travelling movements with

changes in direction and level, both with and without equipment (e.g., selecting two ways to travel on a bench while performing a change in direction and level);

— travel in various ways, and dodge stationary objects or opponents;

Manipulation Skills:

— throw a ball overhead using two hands, while stationary, to a large target or a stationary partner;

— catch, while stationary, objects of various sizes and shapes using two hands both above and below the waist (e.g., catch a nerf ball);

— hit a slowly moving object (e.g., a ball or a balloon) using various parts of the body, directing it to a partner or a large target;

Stability Skills:

— jump for distance or height over low objects;

— balance in different positions, using different body parts and levels (e.g., on and off gymnastics equipment, responding to stimuli in creative dance);

— move their bodies in various ways (e.g., over, under, through, and around equipment).

Fundamental Movement Skills: Grade 4

By the end of Grade 4, students will:

— perform the movement skills required to participate in lead-up games, gymnastics, dance, and outdoor pursuits: locomotion/travelling (e.g., sliding, gliding), manipulation (e.g., kicking, trapping), and stability (e.g., putting their weight on different body parts);

— demonstrate the principles of movement in acquiring and then beginning to refine movement skills (e.g., combining directions and levels in sequence).

Locomotion/Travelling Skills:

— combine locomotion/travelling skills in repeatable sequences, incorporating a variety of speeds and levels (e.g., in novelty dances, co-operative games);

Manipulation Skills:

— throw, both while stationary and while moving, a ball using a one-hand overhand motion to a partner or large stationary target, or pass (hand off) and receive an object (e.g., relaying a baton);

— stop an object with the lower part of the body or with a piece of equipment (e.g., trapping a ball or disc with the foot or a piece of equipment);

Stability Skills:

— balance safely in a variety of static positions;

— grip, hang, and swing from equipment;

— jump from a low height, using a variety of turns, shapes, and directions.

Fundamental Movement Skills: Grade 5

By the end of Grade 5, students will:

— perform the movement skills required to participate in games, gymnastics, dance, and outdoor pursuits alone and with others: locomotion/travelling (e.g., running in patterns in game activities), manipulation (e.g., catching, throwing), and stability (e.g., transferring their weight);

— demonstrate the principles of movement while refining their movement skills (e.g., matching the movements of a partner in a sequence).

Locomotion/Travelling Skills:

— perform a combination of locomotion/ travelling movements, incorporating a variety of speeds, in relationship to objects or others (e.g., square dancing, dodging or faking to escape or deceive an opponent);

Manipulation Skills:

— catch, while moving, objects of various sizes and shapes (e.g., balls, Frisbees) using one or two hands;

— use a piece of equipment to send and receive an object to a partner or a target (e.g., propel a ball with a scoop, hit a badminton bird with a racquet, pass a ball using a floor-hockey stick);

— stick-handle an object (e.g., a ball, a disc) while moving in different directions and at different speeds, alone or with a partner;

— hit a ball with various parts of the body (e.g., heading a soccer ball);

Stability Skills:

— perform a sequence of movements (e.g., rolling, balancing, jumping, landing);

— perform rotations, both single rolls and rolls in sequence, in a variety of directions on mats;

— transfer body weight in a variety of ways, using changes in direction and speed;

— dismount safely from equipment (e.g., from a bench or box-horse).

Fundamental Movement Skills: Grade 6

By the end of Grade 6, students will:

— perform movement skills in the kind of combinations that are required in a variety of modified games, gymnastics, dance, and outdoor pursuits: locomotion/travelling (e.g., running, jumping, and hopping in combination, as performed in basketball or in a triple jump), manipulation (e.g., stepping sideways to get in position to bump or volley a ball, as performed in volleyball), and stability (e.g., running and jumping and landing, as in long jump);

— demonstrate the principles of movement while refining movement skills (e.g., combining body shapes and movements with changes in direction as in a dance or gymnastics routine).

Locomotion/Travelling Skills:

— perform a combination of locomotion/ travelling skills using equipment (e.g., navigating through obstacle courses, skiing, skating);

— demonstrate a variety of running techniques (e.g., sprints, cross-country runs);

Manipulation Skills:

— kick balls of various sizes and shapes for distance and accuracy (e.g., punt a football, kick a soccer ball);

— throw an object overhand or side arm, using the dominant hand, to a target or a partner for distance and accuracy;

— demonstrate goal-tending skills (e.g., blocking, trapping, catching, clearing) with or without a piece of equipment;

Stability Skills:

— jump for height (e.g., vertical wall jump);

— perform locomotion/travelling and stability skills in combination (e.g., use a sprint approach and jump for distance, as in long jump);

— perform a variety of springing actions (e.g., spring into vertical rotations such as quarter-turns on the floor or springs to mounts on equipment).

Importance of Physical Education

Physical education is an integral part of the total education of the child and virtually every state, district, and school in the United States requires physical education for its students. Quality physical education programs are needed to increase the physical competence, health-related fitness, self-esteem, and enjoyment of physical activity for all students so that they can be physically active for a lifetime. Knowing that physical activity promotes health is not enough: students must be given opportunities to gain the knowledge and skills needed to adopt active lifestyles. Physical education teaches students how to add the habit of physical activity into their daily lives by aligning instruction with the National Standards for Physical Education, and by providing content and learning experiences that develop the skills and desire to be active for life.

Values of Physical Activity

Physical activity improves muscular strength and endurance, flexibility, and cardiovascular endurance, as well as serves as a vehicle that helps children establish self-esteem and strive for achievable, personal goals. The Surgeon General's report, Physical Activity and Health concludes that regular moderate physical activity can substantially reduce the risk of developing or dying from heart disease, diabetes, colon cancer, and high blood pressure.

The American Heart Association recommends that all children aged 5 years or older should engage in at least 30 minutes of daily physical activity at a moderate intensity and vigorous physical activity for 30 minutes at least 3 days per week. Acknowledgment of the contributions of school physical education to health led to the inclusion of two national objectives that are related to school physical education in Healthy People 2000, the U.S. Department of Health and Human Services national health objectives:

- Objective 1.8--Increase to at least 50% the proportion of children and adolescents in grades 1-12 who participate in daily school physical education.
- Objective 1.9--Increase to at least 50% the proportion of school physical education class time that students spend being physically active, preferably engaged in lifetime physical activities.

The Surgeon General's report calls school-based physical education "the most widely available resource for promoting physical activity among young people in the United States," and recommends that "every effort should be made to encourage schools to require daily physical education in each grade and to promote physical activities that can be enjoyed throughout life."

National Standards for Physical Education(NASPE)

In 1986, the National Association for Sport and Physical Education (NASPE) appointed its Outcomes Committee to answer the question, "What should physically educated students know and be able to do?" The result of the Outcomes Project was a definition that includes five major focus areas, specifying that a physically educated person:

- has learned skills necessary to perform a variety of physical activities,
- is physically fit,
- participates regularly in physical activity,
- knows the implications of and the benefits from involvement in physical activities,
- values physical activity and its contribution to a healthful lifestyle (National Association for Sport and Physical Education [NASPE].

Following the work of the Outcomes Committee, a Standards and Assessment Task Force was appointed to develop content standards and assessment material based on the previous work. The standards document developed by this group had the following purposes:

— to establish content standards for the physical education school program that clearly identify consensus statements related to what a student should know and be able to do as a result of a quality physical education program; and

— to establish teacher-friendly guidelines for assessment of the content standards that are consistent with instructionally integrated orientations toward the role of assessment in teaching and learning.

In "Moving into the Future: National Standards for Physical Education, A Guide to Content and Assessment," a general description of each content standard is first presented, followed by presentation of the standards according to grade level: K, 2, 4, 6, 8, 10, and 12. Within each grade level, the standard is further defined, followed by a listing of the key points of emphasis for that grade level. Sample performance benchmarks, which describe developmentally appropriate behaviors representative of progress toward achieving the standard, are also presented. Lastly, a variety of assessment techniques appropriate for assessing student achievement of the specified content standard is described. The National Standards for Physical Education indicate that a physically educated student:

1. Demonstrates competency in many movement forms and proficiency in a few movement forms.
2. Applies involvement concepts and principles to the learning and development of motor skills.
3. Exhibits a physically active lifestyle.
4. Achieves and maintains a health-enhancing level of physical fitness.
5. Demonstrates responsible personal and social behaviour in physical activity settings..

6. Demonstrates understanding and respect for differences among people in physical activity settings.
7. Understands that physical activity provides opportunities for enjoyment, challenge, self-expression, and social interaction.

Since 1850, when the first physical training of students in schools began, the emphasis of school physical education has expanded from physical training and calisthenics to performance-related fitness and the development of competitive sports skills. Today the focus of contemporary physical education is on health-related fitness and the behavioural competencies and motor skills needed for lifelong engagement in healthy and satisfying physical activity. A quality physical education curriculum includes:

— mastery of basic skills and understanding of motor skills related to a variety of physical activities so that each individual can make positive decisions about physical activity choices;

— experiences that encourage children to question, integrate, analyze, communicate, and apply cognitive concepts about motor skill and physical activity;

— opportunities to improve social and cooperative skills, and gain a respect and appreciation for diversity; and

— use of fitness education and assessment to help children understand, enjoy, improve, and/or maintain their physical health and well-being.

Implications for Instruction and Programme Support

To maximize the opportunities to learn in physical education, a range of factors must be available. These include time in the schedule, reasonable class size, adequate facilities and equipment, a well-planned curriculum, appropriate assessment procedures, qualified teachers, and positive administrative support. In the continuing quest to make physical education experiences more personally relevant to children and youth, new developments in learning theories, structuring of subject matter, and new perceptions concerning growth and development must be continuously considered, evaluated, and implemented.

The teacher plays the central role in the success of a physical education program and priority must be given to employing qualified elementary, middle, and secondary school physical education teachers to maximize student learning and achievement. Quality physical education is both developmentally and instructionally appropriate for the specific children being served. Instructionally appropriate physical education incorporates the best known practices, derived from research and experiences in teaching children, into a program that maximizes opportunities for learning and success for all. Students should also use technology in today s physical education classes to explore fitness and motor skill concepts in ways that personalize the curriculum more than ever before.

Heart rate monitors, video and digital photography, computer software, and equipment to measure body composition are a few of the tools made possible by technology. Teacher preparation is critical to successful school physical education programs. NASPE standards for beginning physical education teachers outline standards in nine areas: content knowledge, growth and development, diverse learners, management and motivation, communication, planning and instruction, learner assessment, reflection, and collaboration.

These standards provide the basis for guidelines for professional preparation of physical education teachers who have sound knowledge and understanding of kinesiology (the content of physical education) and are also knowledgeable and skillful in the pedagogy that is needed to transmit this knowledge to students.

Quality physical education programs taught by well-trained physical education specialists play a significant role in promoting the health of children and, ultimately, adults. The National Physical Education Standards provide a framework for structuring programs that will develop physically educated children to help the nation to reach its health goals for children and adults.

Youth Welfare in Physical Education

The Government of India under the Chairmanship of Dr. Hirday Nath Kunzru set up a Committee to make recommendations on the coordination and integration of schemes operating in the field of Physical Education, Recreation and Youth Welfare. The Committee submitted its report in December, 1963. One of the important recommendations made by this Committee is that at the school stage there should be an Integrated Programme woven into the fabric of educational system and consisting broadly of a basic curriculum compulsory for all and an optional curriculum.

The basic curriculum should include a minimum programme of physical and cultural activities and the optional part should consist of activities like scouting, montaineering, sports, dance, drama, music, hobbies, social service, workshop activities. This recommendation has been fully accepted by the Government of India and an integrated programme has been worked out in consultation with the experts and it is proposed to launch this integrated programme in all middle, high and higher secondary schools in the country from the next academic year. The new programme will be known as the 'National Fitness Corps.'

National Fitness Corps Programme: This programme is proposed to be launched from the next academic year and will replace the existing programmes under the Physical Education, A.C.C. and National Discipline Scheme. This programme, broadbased as it is, emphasises activities like sports and games, and fuses together all the good features of other programmes which it seeks to replace. Full details about the working of the National Fitness Corps programme are being worked out in consultation with the State Governments etc.

By the end of the financial year 1964-65 about 6500 NDS Instructors will be in position. Besides, about 5000 of the existing In-service Physical Education teachers will receive reorientation training by that period. It is proposed to transfer all NDS Instructors to the States as soon as possible after the launching of the National Fitness Corps programme. Thus, while instructional staff will be under the States, the Central Directorate will confine its role to guidance, coordination, training and other activities which will ensure uniform implementation of the programme. Necessary financial assistance is proposed to be rendered to the States for the introduction of the new programme in all schools. The funds provided for the National Discipline Schemes in 1965-66 budget will be utilised for the impementation of the National Fitness Corps.

Lakshmibai College of Physical Education, Gwalior is progressively expanding its activities. The admissions to the 3-year degree course as well as to the 2-year post-graduate and master's degree course during the year have been the highest so far. 74 students were admitted to the first year degree course and 14 to master's degree course. 7 students, passed the M.P.E. (Part I) examination and 45 the B.P.E. (Final) examination during 1964.

During the year, the College introduced a new two year M.A. (Recreation) Course from the year 1971-72 for training of leaders in Recreation. For the academic year 1971-72, 85 students, including 13 girls, were admitted to the Part 1 of the 3 year Bachelor of Physical Education Course and 14 students including 2 girls, were admitted to the Master of Physical Education Course. Besides these, 7 students were admitted to the Firm year M.A. (Recreation) Course. With these admissions the College has now a total student strength of 249 students, out of whom 36 are girls.

General K. M. Cariappa has been renominated Chairman of the Board of Governors of the College for another term of 3 years. By the end of the year 1965-66, it is hoped that the construction of the swimming pool and two gymnasia-one for men and the other for women students at the College will be completed. The Union Ministry of Education set up an Evaluation Commit- tee to assess the working of the College with a view to finding if the expenditure incurred on the College was justified and also to make recommendations for its future development. This Committee has confirmed that the institution had been fulfilling the purpose for which it was established. Besides, the Committee has made a number of useful recommendations for the development of the College.

National Physical Efficiency Drive was organised all over the country in November, 1964. About 4,800 testing centres were set up and as the information so far available indicates, about 10 lakh persons as aganist 6 lakh in the previous year, participated in the drive. Financial assistance has been given to States to set up about 150 permanent testing centres where facilities and guidance will be available throughout the year to the prospective competitors to improve upon their performance in the various test items.

The Fourth All-India Competition for the National Awards in Physical Efficiency is being organised in February, 1965, at Bangalore. Grants-in-Aid to Private Physical Education Training Institutions 6. projects of hostels or/and administrative blocks of 5 institutions have been approved during the year involving Union Government's contribution or about Rs. 4.5 lakh as aganist the total estimated construction cost of about Rs. 8 lakh. In addition, further assistance has also been extended for the projects of gymnasia approved in the previous years but not yet completed. A total expenditure of about Rs. 4 lakh is expected to be incurred under the scheme during 1964-65. Assistance on the same pattern is expected to be continued during 1965-66 and quite a good number of projects in progress at present are expected to be completed next year.

Promotion of Research in Special Branches of Physical Education Including Yoga Scheme consists of the four main items as given in the paragraphs that follow. While the Lakshmibai College of Physical Education at Gwalior is considering the setting up of a Department of Yoga in the College, the grant-in-aid to the Vishwayatam Yoga Ashram has been stopped on complaints. The Kaivalayadham Shreeman Madhava Yoga Mandir Samiti, Lonavala received grants amounting to Rs. 46,767 from the Ministry during 1964-65 for their scientific research and philosophico-literary research department. The project of the Yoga Institute, Santa Cruz, Bombay, to undertake a survey of the Yogic Institutions in the country with the Union Government's assistance has been approved.

Besides 9 research projects already approved for assistance during the year 1963-64 and which are progressing, some fresh proposals have been received. These will be examined in consultation with the Research Sub-Committee of the Central Advisory Board of Physical Education and Recreation.

Duke of Edinburgh Award Scheme initiated in the U.K. and later put into operation in a number of other Commonwealth countries, the scheme aims at promoting active and creative use of leisure among boys between 14 and 19 years and girls between 14 and 20 years of age. The activities include rescue and public service, expedition, pursuits and interests and fitness etc. The winners get three graded standards of awards in the form of certificates and also medals. It has been decided to extend the scope of the scheme to cover such institutions in India as are desirous of participating in the competitions.

Central Advisory Board of Physical Education & Recreation at its meeting held in May 1964 approved the Integrated Programme of Physical Education and National Discipline which is the basis for the new National Fitness Corps programme. The three-year term of the Board expired in December, 1964 and its reconstitution is under examination. It is proposed to make certain changes in the constitution of the Board, keeping in view the changes that have recently taken place in the field of Physical Education.

The 9th Inter-University Youth Festival was inaugurated by the Prime Minister, Shri Lal Bahadur Shastri at New Delhi on the 14th November, 1964. Forty-seven universities with 610 participants (including 210 women) participated in this Festival. The strength of the contingent from each university was reduced from 24 to 14 students to cut down the expenditure on the Festival.The programme of the Festival included a symposium on the different facets of Jawaharlal Nehru, Shakespearian, recitation, discussions and debates, dance, drama and music and play-day activities. An exhibition hockey match between the Olympic XI and the, Universities XI was also held. The Olympic XI won by a narrow margin of 1 goal.

The various universities also organised Inter-Collegiate Youth Festivals to select their contingent for participation in the Inter-University Youth Festival. Grants were provided by the Ministry for this purpose, to meet 50 per cent of the expenditure subject to a ceiling of Rs. 5,000 for the affiliating university and Rs. 1,000 for residential university.

Under this scheme, students of the age-group 5-24 are given assistance to meet rail/bus fare at students' concession rates subject to a maximum of Rs. 60 per student to enable them to undertake educational tours to places of cultural, historical or educational interest. While two educational institutions of Delhi have been given grant of Rs. 3,061,7 other institutions in the Union Territory of Delhi have been accorded administrative approval for undertaking the tours. The implementation of the scheme in different States is held up as the amounts could not be allocated to the State Governments for want of certain basic statistical information. The likely expenditure on the scheme for the year 1964-65 is Rs. 0.80 lakh.

Youth Hostels: The revised Youth Hostels scheme is under consideration of the Ministry of Finance. An amount of Rs. 20,000 has been released for the Youth Hostel at Always under the old scheme. The likely expenditure for the year 1964-65 is Rs. 0.40 lakh.

Youth Welfare Boards & Committees: 16 universities receiving grants under the scheme have set up youth welfare committees to look after the welfare activities of university youths. A sum of Rs. 42,188 has so far been sanctioned to different universities during the year. Two more universities have submitted their proposals for setting up such committees. The likely expenditure for the year 1964- 65 is Rs. 0.50 lakh.

Youth Leadership and Dramatic Training Camps: These camps are designed to impart short term training to college/ university teachers in the organisation of youth welfare programmes in their respective colleges/ universities. Financial assistance is also given to individual universities to conduct similar camps and the grants cover 75 per cent of the expenditure on admissible items subject to a maximum of Rs. 3,000 for each camp. Requests for such grants have been received from 6 universities. The likely expenditure on the entire scheme during the year 1964-65 is Rs. 0.60 lakh.

N.C.C./A.C.C.: Compulsory N.C.C. training for all able bodied students is in progress. N.C.C. Directorate is the controlling authority for the implementation of the N.C.C. scheme and the Ministry of Defence shares the expenditure with the State Governments.

Circus: There is no budget provision available for this scheme. The Education Ministry only recommends the applications received from the Circus Companies, affiliated to the Circus Federation of India, to the Railway authorities for travel concessions and the State Governments for the grant of camping facilities.

Deputation of Youth Delegations to Various Conferences Abroad. This Ministry does not have any budget provision to finance delegations of youth going abroad for participation in various international conferences/seminars. Two delegations, however, have permitted to participate in the following programmes : (i) a students delegation of 8 members sponsored by the National Council of University Students of India for giving cultural performances in Western European countries for about 2 months. (ii) a delegation of 6 persons (4 from the Y.M.C.A., and 2 from Young Farmers Association of India) for the World Youth Camp held at Tokyo during October, 1964.

Bharat Scouts and Guides

The Government continued to extend financial assistance to the Bharat Scouts & Guides for their various activities. An amount of Rs. 2.20 lakh has already been given to the Bharat Scouts & Guides so far. The likely expenditure for the year 1964-65 is Rs. 2.88 lakh. Besides its usual activities, the Bharat Scouts & Guides participated in the following international conferences/seminars /jamborees : (i) East West Conference at New Delhi. (ii) International Children's Camp at Aztec in Crimea (U.S.S.R.) in August, 1964, (iii) Seventh Australian Jamboree (iv) Golden Jubilee Jamboree at Lagos. The Bharat Scouts & Guides also conducted/organised: (a) Fourth all-India Jamboree at Allahabad in December, 1964. (b) A mountaineering expedition to Mrigthuni by the Girl Guides who successfully climbed the peak.

Labour and Social Service Scheme: This Scheme has been in operation from the fourth year of the first Five-Year Plan. It is divided into two parts : (a) Labour and Social Service camps and (b) Campus Work Projects.

(a) *Labour and Social Service Camps:* The scheme is operated through the agencies of universities, State Governments, the N.C.C. Directorate and voluntary organisations of All-India status like the Bharat Sevak Samaj, Bharat Scouts and Guides and Y.M.C.A. The object of such camps is to inculcate a sense of dignity in manual labour among students and other youths and to give them an opportunity of coming into contact with village life and participating in works of Community Development Blocks.

Each camper is expected to put in about four hours of Shramdan daily in a camp lasting 10 to 30 days on certain selected minor projects. Out of the budget provision of Rs. 8 lakh which has been reduced to Rs. 6 lakh after imposition of an economy cut of Rs. 2 lakh. a sum of Rs. 3,71,569.31 paise was sanctioned to various agencies for holding 191 Labour and Social Service Camps during the period 1st April, 1964 to 15th February, 1965. More proposals for camps are being received. It is anticipated that the entire budget provision will be utilised. A Committee for Coordination of various schemes in the field of physical education, youth welfare etc. was constituted under the chairmanship of Pandit H.N. Kunzru on the 26th May, 1959 which inter alia examined the scheme of Labour and Social Service Camps. In the light of the recommendations made by the Committee in its Report in December, 1963 it has been decided that the educational institutions will be fully responsible for organising and running Labour and Social Service Camps.

(b) *Campus Work Projects*:-The purpose of this scheme is to provide much needed amenities like recreation hall-cum-auditoria, swimming pools, gymnasia, open-air-theatres, pavilions, small stadia and cinder tracks in educational institutions. One of the conditions of grants for the purpose is that the staff and students of the beneficiary educational institutions should offer skilled and unskilled labour on the projects in addition to contributing 25 per cent or more of the actual expenditure on the project.

The grants are paid in three or four instalments depending upon the progress of construction work. An economy cut of Rs. 5 lakh has been imposed on the budget provision of Rs. 15 lakh. Out of the reduced budget provision of Rs. 10 lakh, a sum of Rs. 4.74 lakh was sanctioned for 65 continuing projects during the period 1st April, 1964 to 15th February, 1965. It is anticipated that the entire amount of Rs. 10 lakh will be utilised during the year. Owing to the economy cut, no grant has been sanctioned for new projects under the scheme. It is, however, proposed to revive the scheme during the next financial year and cover the applications invited during this year.

The scheme has been slightly modified so as to cover the setting up of Rifle Shooting Ranges in the educational institutions where Junior N.C.C. is already functioning.

Financial assistance up to a maximum amount of Rs. 1,800 per range will be sanctioned for about 400 such ranges during the years 1964-65 and 1965-66. 50 per cent of the provision for the purpose will be forthcoming from the National Defence Fund.

Cultural Activities

In the field of cultural activities, the Union Government since independence not only maintained and developed the institutions of national importance that were already in existence, but also set up a few new institutions to help maintain and develop the country's valuable cultural heritage as well as to promote cultural unity and emotional integration of the country. Housed in a building known as Rabindra Bhavan in New Delhi, the three Akademis which were set up through Government Resolution and have since become autonomous bodies carry on extensive programme in arts, letters, dance, drama and music.

A Committee under the Chairmanship of Dr. H. J. Bhaba, Chairman, Atomic Energy Commission, was set up in March, 1964 to review the working of the three National Akademis and the Indian Council for Cultural Relations. The Committee has since submitted its report which is under consideration of the Union Government. In addition, the Union Ministry also implements a few programmes to assist the State Governments. and private organisations in the fields.

National Akademis

Lalit Kala Akademi: The Lalit Kala Akademi was set up to foster and coordinate activities in the sphere of visual and plastic arts and to promote thereby the cultural unity of the country. Inaugurated in August, 1954, the Akademi is now registered as a Society under the Societies Registration Act, 1860, and functions as an autonomous organisation, entirely financed by the Union Government. Centering round the promotion of Visual and plastic arts, the main programme of the Akademi consists of organising exhibitions, bringing out publications, granting recognition and financial assistance to art organisations, copying frescoes, and giving awards to arists. The activities of the Akademi during the year are outlined in the paragraphs that follow:

*Exhibitions:*In collaboration with the Max Mueller Bhavan, New Delhi, the Akademi organised at its gallery, the Bahaus Exhibition, depicting through photographs, prints, etc., the story of a movement in Germany which aimed at an integrated development of fine and applied arts and of architecture. The Akademi presented another exhibition of the fresco copies made so far by different artists. Maps, charts and notes were also placed along with the copies, to give a clear idea to the visitors about the location and historical background of the places from which the copies were made-Badami, Sittanvasal, Kulu, Amber, Bairath and Bagh. The National Exhibition of Art will be held some time in February, 1965.

Awards and Fellowships: The Akademi gave ten awards and three Fellowships, one each for sculptor, painter and art historian, during the year 1964.

Publications: Printing of Lalit Kala Contemporary Journal No. 2 has been completed. The Akademi also planned new portfolios which are expected to be ready soon along with the monograph oil Dhanraj Bhagat.

Conference: Artists from all over India met at Hyderabad for a three-day conference, to discuss various problems of mutual interest in January, 1965. Besides the given theme of "New Visions in Contemporary Art", the artists also had deliberations on the Indian National Committee of the International Association of Plastic Arts and its activities, as also on the possibility of co-operation between artists and architects.

*Camp:*The second Sculptors' Camp started at Mahabalipuram on January 18, 1965 will continue till the end of February. Besides about eight sculptors invited directly by the Akademi, a few more are expected to attend as observers, sponsored by different State Akademis. Like the earlier such programme at Makrana (Jaipur) in 1962, the Camp with participants drawn from all over India is sure to create a new stimulus and interest in the contemporary Indian sculpture.

Copying of Frescoes: Tira-Ṣujanpur (Kangra), where copies are to be made next, has already been inspected and preliminary investigations completed. Work, at least in part,will begin soon and is expected to be over by next March.

Visitor from Abroad: Mr. Parsamyan, an artist, critic and Secretary of the Board of Painters (U.S.S.R.), on arrival in the country, pursued a three-week programme implemented by the Akademi under the Indo-Soviet Cultural Exchange proposals.

Grants-in-aid to Recognised Art Societies and State Akademis: Grants totalling Rs. 1,21,500 have been sanctioned to institutions and State Akademis.

*Programmes for 1965-66:*Programmes for 1965-66 will be on lines more or less similar to those followed in previous years. However, mention may be made of the following in particular :

(a) The Akademi is expecting a collection of contemporary British sculpture to be shown at four or five centres in India.

(b) India will be participating, through the Akademi, at 1965 Biennials in Paris and Sao Paulo.

(c) The de-protected monument, Bistidari Malcha, on the Ridge, Delhi, is likely to be put to regular use by artists, as working studios during the next working year.

*Sahitya Akademi:*The Sahitya Akademi, financed wholly by the Union Government was set up to work actively for the development of Indian letters and to set high literacy standards, to foster and co- ordinate literarary activities in all the Indian languages and to promote through them all, the cultural unity of the country. Formally inaugurated on 12th March, 1954, the Akademi was subsequently registered as a Society under the Societies Registration Act, 1860. The programme of the Akademi is mainly directed to meet the challenge posed by an anamoly of the multi-lingual Indian society that while Indian literature is one, writers and readers in one language hardly know anything of what is being written in other languages in the country.

The Akademi, therefore, endeavours to devise ways and means whereby Indian writers may come to know one another across the barriers of language and script and where by the readers may gain access to the variety and complexity of the country's literary heritage. The programme adopted by the Akademi to meet his need comprises several significant activities.

Sangeet Natak Akademi: Like the other two Akademis, the Sangeet Natak Akademi was also set up to foster and develop Indian dance, drama and music and to promote through them the cultural unity of the country. Formally inaugurated in January, 1953, it is now registered as a Society under the Societies Registration Act, 1860. It is wholly financed by the Union Government. The main programme of the Akademi consists of coordinating the activities of State Akademis, promoting research in the fields of dance, drama and music, granting recognition and financial assistance to the institutions working in the fields, bringing out publications and giving awards to artists. The main activities of the Akademi during 1964-65 are described in the paragraphs that follow :

Awards and Fellowships

The Akademi at a ceremony presided over by the President, conferred Fellowships on six artists including one woman and presented awards-3 in music for Karnatak Vocal, Karnatak Instrumental and Hindustani Vocal; 4 in Dance for Bharatanatyam, Kathak, Chakiar Koothu and Yakshagana and 2 in Drama for Drama Direction and Acting in Marathi.

Besides, three plays in Gujarati, Marathi and Telugu were awarded prizes.

Cultural Programmes

(i) *Lectures and Talks:* Foreign dignitaries like Dr. M. M. Barkechli, Director, National Conservatoire of Music, Teheran, delivered a lecture on the Music of Iran on the 11th August, 1964. A series of three lectures, illustrated by tape and disc recording were delivered by Mr. Roger Ashton on the Music of Uzbekistan, Tadzhikistan and Iran, Music of Turkey and Egypt and Music of Tunisia and Morocco. An illustrated talk on Mexican Folk Music was given by Mrs. Margit Alatorre at Rabindra Bhawan on the 25th November, 1964.

(ii) The Akademi jointly with the Siddhendra Kalakshetram, Kuchipudi celebrated the 301st Jayanti of Kshetragna, at Movva and the 550th Jayanti of Siddhendra at Kuchipudi.

(iii) The Akademi also arranged various cultural items including playback of recorded music of Jean Philippe Rameau, recital of the Compositions of Ramnad Srinivasa Iyengar and Bharatanatyam dance by Smt. M. K. Saroja during the year.

(iv) The Sangeet Natak Akademi in collaboration with Sahitya Akademi sponsored a Seminar on Shakespeare on the occasion of Quater- Centenary The seminar was inaugurated by the President at New Delhi. The programme included staging of famous Shakespearean dramas in English Urdu and Bengali by the New Shakespeare Company, London and other dramatic organisations.

(v) On the 5th January, 1965 the Sangeet Natak Akademi jointly with the Royal Netherlands Embassy in India presented a dramatic rendering by Nel Oosthout, the famous Dutch actress, of `Chandalika' by Tagore and `Rebel in Chains' by Theun De Vries.

(vi) A recital of Kuchipudi dance by Vedantam Satyanarain Sarma and his group and an exhibition of musical instruments belonging to the family of Ustad Vilayat Khan, will be organised in Delhi before the end the year.

(vii) The National School of Drama and Asian Theatre Institute staged Strindberg's `The Father' and `Oedipus Rex' in September, 1964.

Special Meeting: A meeting of the Chairman of the State Sangeet Natak Akademis was held under the chairmanship of H. H. Maharaja Shri Jaya Chamaraja Wadiyar Bahadur at Ootacamund on 25th September, 1964 to discuss, among others, measures to be taken for co- ordination of the activities of the State Akademis with the Central Sangeet Natak Akademi.

Participation in International Conferences: The Secretary of the Akademi represented India at a conference on Arab Music organised by the Government of Iraq held at Baghdad in November, 1964.

Institutions run by the Akademi: The Sangeet Natak Akademi runs two institutions, namely, (1) The National School of Drama and Asian Theatre Institute, New Delhi and (ii) The Manipuri Dance College, Imphal.

State Governments, Organisations /Individual Workers

Cultural Exchanges: The main objects of the three schemes covered under this programme, are to promote cultural cultural and emotional integration of the country and provide opportunities to the people of a State to get an idea of the cultural heritage of the people of other States and to provide entertainment to the Armed Forces on India's frontiers. The three schemes are :

*Inter-State Exchange of Cultural Troupes:*Under this scheme, troupes from 13 States visited other States during 1963-64 and in all 25 visits took place. During 1964-65, a troupe each from

Andhra Pradesh, Assam, Jammu and Kashmir, Kerala and Maharashtra visited two other States till December, 1964. Troupes from Manipur, Uttar Pradesh, Bihar, Madras and West Bengal are expected to visit two other States each by the end of March, 1965.

Cultural Exchanges of Outstanding Artists/Troupes Amongst the Zones of India: The performances under this Scheme are arranged directly by the State Governments and the visits are normally reported to the Government of India if a State Government claims the grant admissible under the Scheme to cover the deficit on arranging the performances or when any artists not covered by the scheme is invited to give performances. Intimation has been so far received of a performance in Jammu and Kashmir.

Sponsoring of Cultural Troupes for the Entertainment of Armed Forces in the Forward Areas: Troupes sponsored by the States of Andhra Pradesh, Maharashtra, Orissa and Punjab visited forward areas till the end of December, 1964. A troupe from Delhi sponsored directly by the Ministry of Education also visited the forward areas. Some more visits are likely to take place before March, 1965.

Promotion of Drama Movement in the Country: The Ministry's schemes : (i) Assistance to theatres for the production of new plays; (ii) Study travel grants to theatre groups; (iii) Professional training to qualified students who take to drama; and (iv) Maintenance grants to theatre groups, which were in operation during the past few years on experimental basis were reviewed with a view to examining whether these should continue to operate or these should be replaced by a new comprehensive scheme.

It has been decided to introduce a new scheme in replacement of all or some of the schemes referred to above. Draft of a new scheme has been worked out which is being referred to State Governments for their comments. No fresh grants were, consequently, sanctioned during the year under any one of the old schemes.

Open-Air Theatres in Rural Areas: State Governments are assisted for the construction of 5 open-air theatres per year. A grant of Rs. 1,150 per theatre is sanctioned and this amount is raised to Rs. 1,500 for the theatres constructed in areas receiving heavy rainfall. Since the introduction of the scheme 266 theatres have been sanctioned in various States.

Grants to Cultural Societies/Organisations: Grants are sanctioned on an ad-hoc basis to cultural societies in deserving cases for purposes not covered by the specific schemes or for which no grants is admissible from the National Akademis. Grants totalling Rs. 4,72,000 have been sanctioned up to the end of December, 1964.

Building Grants to Cultural Organisations: Grants are also given to various cultural organisations in the country towards meeting their expenditure on the construction of buildings. So far Rs. 2,07,660 have been sanctioned under this scheme.

Shankar's International Children's Competition: This Competition organised, annually, at the Capital is assisted by the Ministry by way of meeting deficit in the expenditure incurred in arranging the Children's Art Competition, Children's Art Exhibition., On-the-spot Competition, and publication of Children's Art Number and Album, and Prize Distribution on the occasion. The Competition is run by the Children's Book Trust, New Delhi, to whom financial assistance is given by the Ministry for the purpose. During 1964-65 a provision of Rs. 1,25,000 exists.

Financial Assistance to Eminent Artists in Indigent Circumstances: To implement the decision of the Union Government to assist persons distinguished in letters, art and similar other walks of life as may be in indigent circumstances, awards of suitable monthly allowances and or lump sum grants are given by the Ministry under the scheme. There is a lump sum provision for the purpose in India circle of account. First introduced during 1952-53 the scheme was revised in April, 1961. Under the revised scheme the State Governments and the Central Government share the expenditure in the proportion of 1:2. During the year 154 fresh grants have been given under the scheme.

Grants to Literary Institutions: Gants-in-aid to the extent of Rs. 1,17,500 approximately have been paid up to 31 December, 1964 to various institutions engaged in literary activities, towards maintenance, research projects etc.

Strengthening of Existing Institutions: A grant of Rs. 2 lakh has been paid to the Asiatic Society, Calcutta towards completion of its new building.

Grants-in-aid to Individual Research Workers: Under this Ministry's scheme grants-in-aid to individual research workers for fundamental research in Social Sciences and Cultural subjects (subjects not falling under science and technology) financial assistance is extended to scholars (either connected or not connected with any recognised institution) to undertake research work. This scheme was introduced in 1962-63. During the year 1964, grants were given to four research workers.

*Grants-in-aid for Memorials etc.:*Under the scheme assistance is given to institutions engaged in the preservation of buildings, sites and remains Memorials of historical, cultural, scientific, aesthetic and sentimental appeal. Grants amounting to Rs. 89,000 have been sanctioned so far during 1964-65 to various institutions and one State Government for preservation of sites and memorials not protected by the Archaeological Survey of India. Among these a sum of Rs. 50,000 was sanctioned to the Government of West Bengal for repairs to the Burmese Pagoda in the Eden Gardens, Calcutta.

Grants-in-aid to State Governments for the maintenance of Certain Categories of Monuments and for Excavations at approved Sites: Grants-in-aid to some State Governments, amounting to Rs. 68,750 were sanctioned during the current financial year for the maintenance of certain categories of Monuments and also for Excavations. The important item under this scheme is excavations at Yelleshwaram. for which a sum of Rs. 65,000 was sanctioned to the Government of Andhra Pradesh.

Cultural Working Group: In pursuance of the Planning Commission's suggestion a Cultural Working Group was set up in July, 1963, in the erstwhile Ministry of Scientific Research and Cultural Affairs under the Chairmanship of Secretary (Science). The Cultural Working Group met in January, 1964 and two more meetings were held in June, 1964. A preliminary report was prepared and submitted to the Planning Commission, indicating mainly the proposals for the fourth Plan; and in parts a review of what has been done in the cultural fields during the current Plan.

The preliminary report deals with specific schemes which have been formulated. Some of them are schemes which are already being implemented but require to be further expanded to reach larger sections of the population. The emerging pattern of the fourth Plan Cultural Programmes would mean a financial outlay of the order of Rs. 18.67 crore. The existing activities in the field of archaeology will be stepped up. Among other things there are fresh excavations of ancient sites to be undertaken e.g. survey of coast line between the United Arab Republic and of India, as well as setting up of an Institute of Archaeology in Indonesia with which our cultural ties date back to ancient past.

The three National Akademis have now been established them- selves fairly strongly and they are now is a position to extend their activities in the field of dance, drama, music, literature and fine arts.

Museums are yet another effective way of reaching the millions. Statistically there are only 174 museums in the country and majority of them do not receive effective help either by way of financial assistance or expert advice. The proposal suggested will lead to proper development of museums on sound lines.

The schemes under external culture would promote greater harmony with our neighbouring countries and it is hoped through these schemes we will be able to extend the beneficial influences of our culture abroad.

4

Needs and Importance of Physical Education

Physical Education, at least in its origin, has existed since human society. However, it has been a historic category as a whole. Human physical preparation and skill for tools and weapons use in fighting against animals have for centuries played an important role in his survival. Regarding physical education, in ancient times there existed two qualitative modifications; the first being the process of separation of human moving system from the work process and its further improvement and implementation to other fields of human life, the second by the appearance of institutional norms of training and selection, in the period of primitive community decay (ancient times), which became the means of social subjugation of one group of people to another one.

Gradually, physical education was introduced to school education as early as the beginning of the nineteenth century, first as sports activities in private schools for wealthy and privileged class in England, and later as gymnastics and educational institutions on the Continent. In the countries of middle Europe, gymnastics, based on different gymnastics systems, together with other subjects served the goals of old bourgeois school, especially its rigid discipline and militant orientation. What served as main means were formation exercises, simple exercises and exercises on constructed apparatus (horse, horizontal bar, parallel bars), which laid more stressed on mass of forms and its performance (formal characteristics) and less on specific motions and movements and their influence on human body.

The beginnings of physical education in Serbia, with characteristics of military pre-service training, can be traced in the Great Belgrade School in the beginning of the nineteenth century. The first military school in Pozarevac in 1838 had gymnastics in its program. For the first time physical exercises was legislatively introduced in public schools all over Serbia in 1844. It was not earlier than 1863 when the school law paid greater attention to this subject gymnastics or swimming became compulsory. In 1871, gymnastics became a compulsory subject in Serbian primary schools, and in 1882 it became integrated with military exercises in grammar schools.

In the Kingdom of Yugoslavia physical education in schools was neglected both regarding theory and practice. Gymnastics, as a school subject, was included into the subject group of skills., keeping the old attributes from the period of bourgeois school until the end of World War II. Physical Education (PE) training was performed after 'heroic' gymnastic system with traditional forms of folk corporal exercises, the Slavic spirit and tradition, with characteristics of military pre-service training.

After World War II, physical education becomes more and more an integral part of military and of school lives, introducing contemporary pedagogical approach of fresh and brave education teaching concepts, particularly those from the field of didactics, into gymnastics as a school subject. Rigid, artificial and stylized gymnastics forms were more and more replaced by freer devices, such as play, and sports. Instruction moves from indoors to open, outdoors playgrounds, and the number of classes progressively increases, and teachers are becoming professionally educated like other subject teachers.

In other words, the society shows a trend of greater humanization of PE. While the XIX century marked the problem of PE organization within the educational system, the

XX century signified the problem of its realization. The development of PE with the education system was not even in all segments mostly due to the lack of a long-lasting global idea. On the other hand, certain system solutions on micro plan were based upon no previous researches, thus they lacked the exact background, and were only temporary, which badly influenced the pace of constructing PE after a long- lasting concept of education development in general. After World War II, eight primary and secondary school plans and programs of PE were officially accepted. They all represented a pedagogical and educational failure, since the school was caught in the vicious circle of enlightening pedagogy, which primarily believed in knowledge accumulation.

PE was reduced to motor stereotypes acquisition, to acquisition of skills, to accumulation of sports-technical abilities and skills unfit for real life. The subject was shortened both by one class per week, and by a numeric grade, replaced by a descriptive grade. All that contributed that PE became a second-rate subject of less importance. Two conclusions could be drawn out: education reforms dealt more with corrections of the existing system rather than its essential concepts, and that small quantitative remakes of PE curriculum, based on imaginative average will not suffice. If the question of reforms expresses the place and the role of education in the survival of a human community and of an individual in a contemporary society, and if these reforms are viewed as the solution of three great education problems, its structure, its quality and its availability, we can easily conclude that since World War II there has been no real reform, based on previously grounded scientific researches

Development of Physicla Education instruction: Some Experiences

In Russia the end of the XX century signifies the beginning of primary education renewal, which was aimed to radical changes regarding priorities of educational goals. Certain educational standards of primary school has been worked out on two levels: on compulsory minimum of contents (the level of contents presentation), and on the level of students' preparation. Primary goals of PE are to improve health, physical development and to increase work abilities of students, to develop high moral qualities in students, to reinforce the idea that health is not merely an individual, personal matter, to develop and encourage the need for systematic and individual physical exercises, to offer knowledge in regard to hygiene and medicine, to help accept necessary concepts and information from physical culture and sport, and to encourage the development of driving-forward qualities.

PE program content is divided into four segments. They are elementary knowledge (contents which help enlarge the knowledge regarding students own organisms, their hygienic needs, chosen sports activity, human abilities, his culture , and value orientations), general physical preparation (contents with exercises, commands, and other necessary physical activities which influence the formation of motion culture and the development of particular physical qualities), specialized preparation (contents which offer program in basketball, which influences both technical and tactical preparation of students), and estimated indicators of physical preparation (contents which include exercises and tests that measure the level of students preparation).

The assessment of students achievements is determined by the level of his relation towards the improvement, knowledge of basic PE theories, by the way of his physical and specific habits acquisition, and by his ability to solve certain questions regarding personal physical preparation. In Poland, a reformed school plan and program of multi-level education (3+3+3) has been in progress since the end of the XX century. This program is not focused on study subjects, but on student's personality and its developmental requirements as the subject of education. In the first level (classes from I to III) there is no division into study subjects (integral instruction). In the second level (classes IV to VI) instruction is partially divided into subjects with block teaching of some study subjects.

Regarding Physical Education there are 3 classes per week in the second level. The instruction must be correlated to psychophysical development and abilities of children, and does not follow the compulsory concept of full realization of the plan and program, which was the case in the past. After finishing the six years of primary school, students take knowledge and skills examinations in majority of study subjects, not in mother tongue and mathematics only.

In Hungary, framed regulations of instructional plan and program are closely followed by the framed proportions of certain fields of instruction. The study subject Physical Education takes 10 to 14 % of the total instructional period in the week schedule for the first four classes, and 9 to 13 % for the fifth and sixth class. This educational field is in the function of the development of psychosomatic status of children and their interest in play, in enriching their motion ability, as well as in learning and improvement of their motion culture. This implies the development of coordination abilities fit for learning motion activities, sports, with stress on assurance of motion activities, and adjusting motion and problem solving to the abilities of children.

The subject content is divided into four segments. The segments are as follows: healthy corporal development (different life situations, breathing exercises, system music ending of motion activities, and exercises for good body condition); motion culture development (content for acquiring various natural forms of motion in different conditions and different variants); motor skills development (content which influences the development of conditioning and coordinating skills); and maintenance of motion requirements (content of systematic influence on hygienic way of life and on physical activity).

By the end of the XX century, Slovenia introduced the nine-year primary school (principle 3+3+3), with school entrance at the age of six. In the first three years instruction is entrusted to teachers alone, from the fourth to the sixth class both to teachers and subject teachers, while in the last three classes instruction is performed by subject teachers only. Physical (sport) Education is included in all nine years of education with 834 classes (the third largest number, after mother tongue and mathematics). The goals of the subject include optimal physical development and motion (physical) and functional skills development, acquisition of different natural forms of motion, play and sports, gaining pleasure from sport, education for games, and introduction to theoretic information. However, the contents are adjusted to students' age.

In the first two classes, students learn and acquire natural forms of motion and play, athletics, gymnastics, and swimming alphabet, dances, ball games, and go on picnics and tours. Furthermore, in the fourth, fifth, and sixth class, they continue to acquire natural forms of motion with the stress on general condition preparation and games. They learn athletics, gymnastics with rhythmic, dances, basketball, volleyball, handball, small football, swimming, and some water activities, skiing and other winter activities. In addition, they go to picnics and more demanding mountain visits.

In Croatia, there were no changes except that the instructional plan and program was renewed at the end of the XX century. However, the system of lower-grades instruction (classes I to IV) has suffered several alternations. Regarding Physical and Health Education the number of classes per week has been increased. This should reduce the children deficit for motion and sports activities. The goals, objectives and contents of the subject have stayed unchanged, as in Serbia in the last decade of the XX century. The program structure is aimed towards the development of physical activities, sport and technical education and towards connecting physical education with life and work in general.

The contents of the subject include natural forms of motion (walking and running, jumping and over jumping, hitting and catching, pulling and pushing, hanging, etc.), apparatus exercises, ground exercises, balance exercises, games, rhythmic exercises, and folk dances. In the fourth class the contents include athletics and football, and minimal educational demands (assessment) as well.

Comparative analysis shows that years of primary school attendance differs with countries in transition. In Russia it is a four-year primary school, in Poland a six-year school, in Hungary, Croatia, and in Serbia it is an eight-year primary school, while in Slovenia a six-year school . All countries share independent study of mother tongue, mathematics, physical education, art education (visual art and music) and nature and social science study. However, the name for PE differs from country to country.

In Hungary, the name of the subject is Physical Education and Sports, in Slovenia it is Physical (namely Sports) Education, in Croatia Physical and Health Culture, while in Russia, Poland and Serbia the subject is named Physical Education. The quantity of lessons goes from 2 to 3 per week. All transition countries have 3 lessons a week, which is next to mother tongue, literature and mathematics week quantity of lessons, except in Russia, which has 2 lessons per week. The goals of the subject vary from country to country. Nevertheless, they share certain characteristics, such as development of physical abilities, acquisition of motion skills and elementary theoretic knowledge.

Experience of the European Community : Elementary Physical Education

In Germany, different regions have their primary school plans and programs. The objective of Sports and school sports instruction is to help children experience many physical, dynamic and social situations, to develop their physical and spiritual abilities, and to maintain and increase the joy of motion, play, and participation in sports. This multi sport education should fulfill the following goals: acquisition of immediate physical, personal, and material experiences, which are adequate for children; development of social and integrative ways of behavior, development of communal spirit; development of skills in and through sports; and finally, development of ecology and healthy habits and concepts. The instructional contents are divided into four segments: Playing play; Movement and motion with or without apparatus; Motion on big apparatus; Play and motion in water (in the form of individual, couple, or group sports experience).

In France, primary school is organized in cycles, which enable flexible approach concerning differences in children, their needs, expectations and developmental dynamics. Physical and sports education has to enable students to perform more complex activities after each cycle, to estimate the strength of efforts and the influence it has on the organism, to use knowledge and skills effectively in performing physical, and sports activities, to participate in various ways in collective activities and to obey rules, to participate in individual and collective games and to strive for best results, and to be able to evaluate the results. Repeated and satisfactory exercises help development of motor abilities and keep the balance of children activities. The contents of the instruction include different movements play, athletic activities, and gymnastic-like activities, rhythmic, activities with two opponents, swimming activities, traditional, sport and group games, different country activities, and so on.

Different cantons in Switzerland have different plans and programs for primary schools. In schools Sport begins from the fact that there is a human need for motion and that play and games give pleasure to children. Instruction of sports, whose goal is to educate and train students in useful sports activities, helps children understand their sport as sense full action. The basic elements of sports instruction are: perception, sense of body, health, impression, experience, sensation, expression, esthetics, formation, efficacy, training, activity, competition, test, comparison, tension, drama, adventure, communal spirit, sociability, and making friends. The instructional contents are: taking care of one's own body, scenic presentation, dance; balancing, climbing, turning over, fight, running, jumping, throwing; play, sport in the open, and broader tasks. Different series of motion tests are used to asses the achieved results, together with tests for swimming sports, and gymnastics and sports achievements.

A careful comparative analysis indicates the variety of primary school duration in the European Community countries. In Germany, this is a four-year school, in France a five-year school, while Switzerland has a six-year primary school. The subject itself has different names and different number of lessons per a week. In Germany and Switzerland the subject is named Sport, while in France it is Physical and Sport Education. The number of lessons per week varies from 2 in Switzerland, 3 in Germany and even 6 in France (art lessons included) for the first two years (the cycle of substantial knowledge) and 5 lessons plus 30 minutes from III to V class (the cycle of curriculum deepening).

If we bear in mind and take into consideration different experiences of the transition countries and European Community countries, we could say that the development of primary PE plans and programs at the beginning of the XXI century should, before all aim towards redefining (goals and purposes) of this education field. The reason for this could be found in the false definition of the subject goal, although we deal with a common idea (purpose) of PE, which says why something is being done in our pedagogical work, but they are not the synonyms. Goals tell us about what and to what extent students should achieve something (abilities) or master something (skills). The very purpose of PE brings out the contents and goals, which, in addition, bring out work methods and ways of evaluation. The purpose should be viewed as a long-term educational ideal, an idea, or a directive we strive to achieve, while goal is a short-term educational intention, which is exact and (operatively) determined, and as such easy to achieve directly, to measure and to justify.

The goal is both qualitative and quantitative human value, which should be achieved. This is why a redefined. Purpose of Physical Education is to contribute to the integral development of student's personality (cognitive, affective, and motor), by using various systematic motor activities, in correlation with other fields of education. This especially means the development of motor abilities, acquisition and usage of motor skills and habits, and of necessary theoretic knowledge in everyday and specific life and work.

At the same time, our theory and our practice does not recognize instructional, educational, and motion assignments of physical education. They are neither purpose nor aim, but activity, which helps to achieve both. This is why it is necessary to redefine the assignments in regard to the sex and age of students (they should be grouped after different criteria, starting from anatomy and physiology criteria, cinematic, and psychosomatic criteria) into goals of physical education of students regarding lower grades primary school students. bio-psycho-social status.

This includes the following: fulfillment of children elementary need for motion and play, and for competition to some extent (in motivation field); encouraging their growth and development, formation of proper body holding, and prevention and removing of body deformities (in morphology field); development of coordination, flexibility, balance, and explosion power as motor ability components; acquisition of motor skills in all natural (Phil genetic) forms of movements in different situations; elementary games, rhythmic and dancing and ground exercises, introduction with moving abilities and limitations of their body (in motor field); firming and strengthening of their organism and their health, development of hygienic habits (in health field); formation of moral and willing qualities of a person (positive attitude towards work, acceptable forms of behavior, etc. in connatural field); and socialization of students, too.

Considering the redefined aims and goals of Physical Education it is necessary to redefine the PE program, which is divided into three fields: development of physical skills; sport and technical education; and connecting PE with life and work. The primary school PE program contents should be structured into motor activities (means of PE), which should follow thematic fields, such as development of motor skills, acquisition of motor skills and habits, and acquisition of theoretic knowledge.

Restructuring of the contents (i.e. the scope, depth, and order of PE means elementary, accessory and additional) could be very well done by redefining of the program. This means that exercises could be grouped after different criteria; after elementary means criteria (motor activities), after accessory means of PE (buildings, apparatus, and requisites), and after motor abilities criteria (e.g. balance).

Furthermore, the exercises could be redefined into contents (elementary means) of physical education in lower grades of primary school (with 3 lessons of exercises a week), which include organized getting into line and motion (line exercises); body shape exercises; natural forms of motion (elementary Phil genetic motor structures); walking, running, jumping, throwing, crawling, catching, lifting, carrying, pulling, pushing, climbing, hanging, turning over, rolling; elementary games (simple motor games), and later even sport games; rhythmic exercises and children folk dances (dance exercises); floor exercises, bench exercises, and later on even special form of motion, such as athletics, apparatus exercises, skiing, and elements of self-defense.

The validity of the name of the subject itself justifies the meaning of the syntagm .physical education., which has two words. The first word is the adjective physical (natural, made in nature, sensory, corporal), which indicates that a man is nature-gifted, not merely a simple human body, but an integral being (cognitive- affective- motor). Hence there is no dualism between physical and psychological in the name physical education (the theory of soul and body), since each motor activity is a process of the central nervous system.

The second word education means an aimed social and pedagogical process of human individual development. In other words, this is a process of transferring and acquiring of knowledge, skills and habits. Generally speaking, the basic field of physical education is the whole activity of programmed education and anthropology context of physical activities. In order to make PE instruction more rational, it is of great importance to replace the thesis in our education system, which concretely means that plan and program of PE in lower grades of primary school must focus on processing (teaching and training).

In Serbian language, the words which are commonly used to denote teaching and training are very much inadequate. Teachers should focus on students, who should be the subject material for modeling), not the physical exercises and teaching units (motor activities as elementary means of physical education). To make it clearer, certain motion activities physical exercises are not their own goal. They are the means we apply and use in the development of students motor skills and for acquisition of certain motor skills and habits.

Consequently, if the process of physical education is oriented towards teaching students, development of the whole personality and acquisition of motor skills, this process should be dominated by teaching methods (instruction) i.e. synthetic and analytic methods of motor learning. If, on the other hand, this process is generally oriented towards the development of physical and motor abilities acquisition of permanent motion habits and creativity, this process should rest on training methods (drill).

We could easily justify the necessity to have 3+1 PE lesson a week in all classes of primary school (3 lessons of unique compulsory program and 1 compulsory lesson of elective sports activity) from various aspects. First, from the aspect of physical education process (at this age, children need to have permanent, every day physical activity, to restrict them of overloaded school program). Second, from the aspect of motor activities of students (motor deficit, especially present in the period of intensive growth, so that optimal motion regime becomes particularly important at that age). Finally, from the aspect of influence on other features of students.

Inadequate and inefficient number of lessons, the lack of motor activities with students, and disability of daily exercises could be best solved by organization, intensification, and differentiation and individualization of PE instruction in lower grades of primary school.

Regarding re-evaluation of educational process, we should rather asses the development and improvement in the function of psychosomatic status of children than the norm issues. Inspection of achieved goals of physical exercises / physical education process was based upon irregular application of assessment method (a way of evaluation). Since PE is a process through which we aim to develop certain issues (e.g. students' motor abilities) or to acquire (their motor skills), we have to be aware of the fact that nothing but students achievement (improvement) viewed in a certain period of time (e.g. cycle, semester, school-year) is to be assessed, providing that we assess the product of a continuous education work, not the results of genetic code and biological growth and development, which are often wrongly compared to the features of the same population of a country abroad.

The development of education plans and programs of primary school should strive to unload the unneeded and inadequate acquisition of knowledge and skills, the development of features and characteristics of a student's personality which can meet both his and needs of the society. Traditional instruction and its intellectual academic approach show the defect of the concept in which teacher's role is to teach, and student's role is to acquire the contents. This approach reduces PE to mere acquisition of motor stereotypes, and to acquisition of skills, and useless fund of sport technical abilities and skills, which do not have any significant meaning in real life.

Teaching should be modified and altered in such direction to become an active and creative instruction with a student as the central figure of the whole education process, which should lay more stress on its developmental function. Each student has to be regarded as an individual with his own individual features and abilities. To be active means to express one's ability, gifts, and creativity shared by all human beings to some extent. In his educational work, a PE teacher must repeatedly try to give answers to questions like what, when, what with, how much, what for and how to introduce and apply different motor activities into teaching in order to contribute to the integral development of his students personality. He must always keep in mind a motto that. There is no greater inequality than the same treatment of the unequal.

Health Promotion Strategies through Health-Promoting School

Health promotion strategies through a Health-Promoting School to improve the health, education and development of children, families and community members. The Ottawa Charter for Health Promotion and will help people to apply a new approach to public health, one that creates ongoing conditions conducive to health and well-being, as well as reductions in prevailing health concerns.

Environmental conditions, such as technical and societal issues in the school, community and family, might not be ideal and affect the extent to which nutrition interventions can be implemented. However, a Health-Promoting School contributes to improve those conditions by fostering nutrition-related interventions even in a less healthful environment.

What is healthy nutrition?

Healthy nutrition takes many forms and is understood differently in different countries and among different cultures. In general, healthy nutrition should be an integral part of daily life that contributes to the physiological, mental and social well-being of individuals. It is the combined effect of food, health and care. Nutritional well-being is determined by consuming safe food as part of an appropriate and balanced diet that contains adequate amounts of nutrients in relation to bodily requirements. The health and lifestyle of an individual influences the extent to which food contributes to good social, mental and physical well-being. Care is shown by providing time, attention and support in the household and the community to meet the food and health needs of the child and other family members. Furthermore, social ties are validated and maintained by the exchange of food since offering food is associated with offering love, affection and friendship.

What is malnutrition?

Malnutrition is any physical condition resulting either from an inappropriate or inadequate diet, such as a diet that either provides too much or too little of necessary nutrients, or from a physical inability to absorb or metabolize nutrients. Malnutrition can be related to various factors, such as infections which lead to poor appetite and malabsorption, poverty, and lack of access to food, sanitation and/or health services. Malnutrition negatively affects the quality of life and learning as well as death and disease status.

Nutrition interventions are policies, services, learning experiences and other actions implemented by schools, individuals or groups to make healthy nutrition a way of daily life. Nutrition interventions are designed to promote health and decrease the risk of disease. In a Health-Promoting School, nutrition interventions are integrated into all aspects of the school and community life, such as the physical and psychosocial environment; a wide variety of educational opportunities; school/community projects; school health services; health promotion for school staff; counselling and social support programmes; physical exercise, recreation and sport; and food programmes.

Efforts to Improve Nutrition?

Nutrition is vital to all human beings and to the societies that they comprise. Adequately nourished people enjoy optimal growth, health and well-being. Girls in particular benefit from good nutrition as their health status and eating habits have a major impact on pregnancy, lactation and nourishment of their children. While over 800 million people are estimated to lack access to food to meet their daily basic needs for energy and protein, more than 3 billion people are deficient in essential micronutrients such as iodine, vitamin A and iron. Many forms of malnutrition exceed the worldwide incidence of most other diseases. For instance, more than half of the 12.2 million deaths every year of children under the age of 5 in developing countries are associated with malnutrition. Thus, efforts are needed to make healthy nutrition accessible for everyone, everywhere and at all times.

Schools provide the most effective and efficient way to reach large portions of the population, including young people, school personnel, families and community members. Students can be reached at influential stages in their lives, during childhood and adolescence when lifelong nutritional patterns are formed. Children at every successive year from the earliest grade through secondary school can be addressed. Schools have been given the mandate and responsibility to enhance all aspects of development and maturation of children and youth under qualified guidance.

Furthermore, schools also provide a setting to introduce nutrition information and technologies to the community and can lead the community in advocating policies and services that promote good nutrition. No other setting than schools offers these opportunities on as equal a basis. Based on the latest scientific research and programme experiences, it is designed to help people address the broad range of factors that can be modified to implement healthy nutrition as an essential element of a Health-Promoting School.

Good nutrition strengthens the learning potential and wellbeing of children. Good health and nutrition are needed to achieve one's full educational potential because nutrition affects intellectual development and learning ability. Multiple studies report significant findings between the nutritional status and cognitive test scores or school performance. Consistently, children with more adequate diets score higher on tests of factual knowledge than those with less adequate nutrition. For instance, studies in Honduras, Kenya and the Philippines show that the academic performance and mental ability of pupils with good nutritional status are significantly higher than those of pupils with poor nutritional status, independent of family income, school quality and teacher ability.

Good nutrition enables healthy adulthood and ageing

Among well nourished people, acute disease and illness tend to be less frequent, less severe and of shorter duration thus providing increased capacities to perform daily activities. Good nutrition also fosters mental, social and physical well-being throughout life; for instance, by strengthening a positive body image and increasing the sense of personal worth. Healthy nutrition can also contribute to a more comfortable life by helping young people to develop healthy teeth and gums. Thus, good nutrition during childhood helps to lay the foundation for a healthy adulthood.

A healthy diet can also contribute to more mobility in older age. For instance, it is likely that youth is a unique time to acquire the strongest possible bones to decrease the risk of osteoporosis in old age. Diets rich in calcium can help build stronger bones while diets rich in protein and salt increase the chances of losing bone density later in life. Thus, it is important to enable children to establish or reinforce personal skills, healthy perceptions and useful knowledge in nutrition to promote their own health and the health of those they care for. It is beneficial to teach persons healthy eating patterns when they are young since eating patterns are established early in life and are difficult to change once they are developed during youth.

Many of the problems of childbirth, such as haemorrhage, infection and obstructed labour, can be reduced in severity by adequate nutrition earlier in life. For instance, small stature, which may be related to under nutrition, is a well-known risk factor for obstructed labour. Anaemia, which can result from inadequate intake of iron-rich foods, lack of iron supplements or parasite infection, is known to cause about one-fifth of maternal deaths during pregnancy and childbirth.

Women's social roles can also be enhanced through nutrition interventions in areas where women primarily perform the role of preparing food for their families. Increases in women's nutritional knowledge help ensure better preparation, preservation, handling and distribution of foods. Increased capacity to handle their responsibilities can, in turn, enhance women's social and economic status. Thus, ensuring schooling with effective nutrition interventions for young girls can be one of the most important and effective means of improving women's nutrition and health status because of the associated effects on health, fertility and social development.

Healthy nutrition contributes to decreasing today's leading health problems

Studies show that early indicators of chronic disease begin in youth. For instance, avoiding obesity in childhood and youth is important because once attained, obesity tends to continue in adulthood, contributing to chronic diseases. Furthermore, the hardening of arteries and high blood cholesterol levels, which make a major contribution to coronary heart disease, are influenced by nutrition and lifestyle. Thus, adequate nutrition and physical activity are likely to have long-term health benefits in reducing the growing number of diet-related, non-communicable diseases.

— Obesity in infants, children and adults is a major problem worldwide. The prevalence of obesity in adults is 10% to 25% in most countries of Western Europe, 20% to 25% in some countries in the Americas, up to 40% in some countries in Eastern Europe, and more than 50% in some countries in the Western Pacific. Obesity rates, which are doubling every 5-10 years in many parts of the world, are placing significant additional financial burdens on health systems to deal with the resulting problems. Obesity will eventually lead to chronic disorders such as diabetes, high blood pressure, high cholesterol levels, hardening of arteries and some forms of cancer. Obesity also leads to acute consequences of chronic disorders including strokes and heart attacks. Reducing caloric intake and increasing physical activity help decrease the risk of obesity.

— Cardiovascular Diseases include coronary heart disease which is a major cause of adult death. The risk of cardiovascular disease can be decreased by healthy eating, especially by consuming a low fat diet.

— Cancer accounts for 25% of all deaths in developed countries. It has been suggested that practicable dietary means could reduce cancer deaths by as much as 35%. Eating a diet that contains plenty of fruit and vegetables in general can significantly reduce the risk of cancer.

— Eating Disorders present serious threats to adolescents' health and can lead to death. Psychological counselling, medical treatment and dietary advice can help to prevent and treat eating disorders.

Nutrition education has been shown to have a significant effect in fostering healthful eating habits. Thus, schools can contribute to reducing these nutrition-related problems by integrating nutrition interventions into a comprehensive approach to school health, as illustrated by the Health-Promoting School.

Good Nutrition Strengthen the Economy

Adequate nutrition is necessary for children to become fit and productive adults, capable of fulfilling their responsibilities in life. People who are well-nourished and educated are clearly more productive and consequently improve their own income as well as their contribution to the national economy. For instance, improvements in health and wellbeing of women and their families through better nutrition contribute to reducing their financial burdens and time constraints. Gained time and resources can be used for income-generating and productive activities or for participating in educational, health or social engagements from which women and their families can benefit.

Furthermore, implementing essential public health programmes, including nutrition and health education and micronutrient supplementation, have been estimated to reduce a considerable amount of the disease burden in low- and middle-income countries. For example, using conservative assumptions, the benefits of investing in school feeding will far exceed the costs even though this is one of the most expensive possible nutrition interventions. In addition, nutrition interventions can contribute to reducing the substantial health care costs for nutrition-related chronic diseases and for productivity losses due to nutrition-related health problems.

Malnutrition affect children's Learning

The education of millions of children throughout the world is being held back by malnutrition. Malnutrition in early childhood can affect school aptitudes, time of school enrolment, concentration and attentiveness. Children with a history of severe malnutrition perform less well on tests of IQ and specific factual knowledge than children in matched comparison groups. Undernourishment also impairs the ability to concentrate, learn and attend school regularly. A child who is malnourished and subsequently suffering from poor health cannot adequately take advantage of instructional and learning materials. Thus, good nutrition is needed to strengthen the learning potential of children, to enable them to learn effectively and maximize investments in education.

Malnutrition is a major factor in 54% of deaths to children under the age of 5 in the developing world. Moreover, 83% of these deaths are attributable to mild-to-moderate, rather than severe, malnutrition. Malnutrition disrupts growth and weakens the mental development of children, leading to less fit and productive adults.

For example:

— Protein-energy malnutrition (PEM) affects about 200 million children worldwide under the age of 5. The actual numbers of protein-energy malnourished children has recently risen in Africa and South-East Asia. Protein-deficient children do not grow at their genetic potential. They also have an increased risk of severe consequences from common childhood infections. Current and prior protein-energy malnutrition has been shown to result in poor retention of factual knowledge, poor school attendance and poor school performance.

— Iron deficiency affects approximately 2 000 million people in developed and developing countries. Iron deficiency anaemia in infants and children can retard physical growth and delay cognitive development as well as increase susceptibility to infection. Furthermore, it impairs the reproductive function of women, which puts the lives of both women and their babies at risk.

— Vitamin A deficiency puts over 250 million children worldwide at risk of blindness. Every year up to one half of a million children become partly or totally blind. Two-thirds of these children die within a few months of going blind. Even moderate levels of deficiency can lead to stunted growth, increased susceptibility and severity of infections and higher death rates. Vitamin A deficiency is the single greatest cause of preventable childhood blindness.

— Iodine deficiency is estimated to affect over 800 million people worldwide. Over 40 million people are affected by some degree of iodine deficiency related brain damage. In later infancy and childhood, iodine deficiency causes mental retardation, delayed motor development, growth failure, stunting, speech and hearing defects.

Iodine deficiency is the single most common preventable cause of mental retardation and brain damage in children.

All of these consequences of malnutrition compromise children's attendance and performance at school. They can be reduced by school-based interventions. Also, educating parents, parents-to-be and other family and community members as well as providing resources to correct deficiencies will help decrease the risk of developing these conditions.

Nutrition interventions improve children's learning and school attendance

Good health and nutrition are needed for concentration, regular school attendance and optimum class performance. Existing research makes a convincing case that nutrition and health interventions will improve school performance. For instance, studies in multiple countries show that the academic performance and mental ability of pupils with good nutritional status are significantly higher than those of pupils with poor nutritional status. This and other evidence of the positive impact of good nutrition has been so convincing that the United Nations Sub-Committee on Nutrition recommends health and nutrition programmes among efforts to increase school enrolment and learning.

Schools are vitally important settings through which to promote good nutrition and provide nutrition interventions

Schools offer more effective, efficient and equal opportunities than any other setting to promote health and healthy eating. They reach young people at a critical age of development in which lifestyles, including eating patterns, are developed, tested and adapted in schools and through social interactions between students, teachers, parents and others. Especially, lower grade levels provide excellent opportunities because eating habits are formed early in life. In addition, schools have the potential to reach not only students but also staff, teachers, parents and community members, including young people not attending school. A Health-Promoting School provides a means to develop and manage nutrition interventions in cooperation with parents and students.

Schools are an ideal setting to promote health and healthy nutrition for several reasons :

— Schools reach a high proportion of children and adolescents.

— Schools provide opportunities to practice healthy eating and food safety.

— Schools can teach students how to resist unhealthy social pressures since eating is a socially learned behaviour that is influenced by social pressures.

— Skilled personnel are available to provide follow-up and guidance - after appropriate training of students, teachers and other service personnel.

— Evaluations show that school-based nutrition education can improve eating behaviours of young persons.

How to improve health and well-being through school nutrition interventions

Evidence for many years has supported that well-managed nutrition education programmes can, at relatively low cost, bring about behaviour changes that contribute to improved nutritional well-being. For instance, studies in the United States have documented that carefully designed and implemented comprehensive health education curricula can prevent certain adverse health behaviours, including dietary patterns that cause disease. Students in behaviourally based health and nutrition education programmes have shown significant favourable changes in blood cholesterol, blood pressure and body fat. Thus, a focus on behaviour is considered a key determinant in the success of nutrition education programmes .

Additionally, school feeding programmes increase food availability to schoolchildren who need adequate food while promoting long-term development through support and education. While studies still continue, numerous evaluations of school feeding programmes have reported either significant increases in height and/or weight for participating children or in attendance and achievement. School feeding programmes also contribute to decrease hunger, which helps children concentrate on their studies.

Schools can provide interventions to improve nutrition in ways that are highly cost-effective

Cost-effective interventions in schools can prevent or greatly reduce health problems and consequences of malnutrition and foster the positive effects of nutrition. Compared with various public health approaches, school health programmes that provide safe and low-cost health service interventions, such as screening and health education, are shown by research to be one of the most cost-effective investments a nation can make to improve health. Furthermore, among the most cost-effective investments in health are programmes that include expanded micronutrient supplementation and increased knowledge about nutrition. Illustratively, a nutrition education programme in Indonesia which was based on behavioural change showed a considerably greater impact at notably lower cost than other types of interventions to which it was compared.

Education and healthy nutrition for girls have a positive impact on the health of families

Improving and expanding educational opportunities for girls is one of the best health and social investments. Improvements to girls' health will in turn improve the health of their children and families because women generally have a major responsibility to care for others within the household. This generally involves household management, food preparation, cleaning duties, obtaining health care, education and supervision of children, all of which can have a significant impact on health.

Furthermore, educated girls are healthier than girls with no or little education. Educated girls and women seek appropriate prenatal care, give birth to healthier babies and bring them home to healthier environments. Research evidence makes it clear that the single most important factor in determining a child's health and nutritional status is its mother's level of education.

Malnourished mothers tend to have low birth weight babies, thus perpetuating the problem of malnutrition and ill health from one generation to the next. For instance, a child's aptitude for formal education may be in jeopardy even prior to school enrolment if the mother suffered from maternal iodine deficiency during pregnancy. Thus, educating young mothers and mothers-to-be is one of the best ways of ensuring the nutritional future of the next generation. In addition, the school system may be particularly useful in trying to supplement the diet of girls before puberty to ensure the remaining growth potential is fully achieved during this critical stage.

Nutrition interventions in schools benefit the entire community

School health education about good nutrition also serves as a means to inform families and other community members about ways to promote wellbeing and prevent malnutrition. For instance, educating children about good eating habits has the potential to enhance the nutrition and health status of their younger siblings whom they may take care of as well as of other family members that learn concomitantly with their children. In addition, involving parents in nutrition interventions at the elementary school level has been shown to enhance the eating behaviour of both students and parents.

Research also shows that school health education interventions can be considerably strengthened by complementary community-wide strategies. Thus, schools can be the centre for community enhancement projects that include programmes to improve the health and nutritional status of the community. Schools also provide a setting to introduce new health information and technologies to the community.

For instance, the establishment of school canteens offering healthy food choices and practising good food safety is a way to demonstrate how to improve facilities in communities. Furthermore, partnerships between schools, organizations and businesses can benefit both the school and the community, if the partnership is mutually beneficial.

Planning the Interventions

Nutrition can be an entry point for building a school's capacity to plan and implement a wide range of health promotion strategies and interventions that will respond to identified needs and contribute to both health and education. Once nutrition is recognized as a priority for both education and health, the next step is to plan the interventions. This can be done by determining which strategies will have the most significant influence on health, education and development and how such interventions can be integrated with other health promotion efforts for maximum results. Interventions should enable students, parents, teachers and community members to make healthy decisions, practice healthy behaviours and create conditions conducive to health.

School and Community Involvement in Planning

Health-Promoting Schools involve members of the school and community in planning programmes that respond to their needs and that can be maintained with available resources and commitments. Two important groups that should be involved in the planning process are a school health team and a community advisory committee.

School health team

A Health-Promoting School should have a designated team to

coordinate and monitor health promotion policies and activities. Since schools should implement programmes that respond to important and relevant community needs, it is essential to involve students, parents, teachers and school management from the beginning in the planning process. When young people are involved early, they can help develop and plan a programme that responds to their specific needs and concerns. Parents and teachers can help ensure that programmes are developed in a culturally appropriate manner. Active participation also builds a sense of ownership of the programme, which enhances its sustainability and support.

Since teachers and other school staff play a key role in carrying out health promotion interventions, their participation is important to ensure that interventions are developed with consideration to what they know and what they can do to establish healthy nutrition as an essential element of a Health-Promoting School. If a school does not have a committee or group organised to address health promotion, the healthy nutrition effort can provide the opportunity to form one.

The team should include a balance of students and adults with various responsibilities in the school who are committed to the idea of health and healthy nutrition. Potential members of the school health team include: teachers, administrators, students, parents and school-based service providers, such as members of food services and health services.

A school health team needs to be designated with responsibility and given time and authority to lead and oversee health promotion efforts in the school. A healthy nutrition task force within that group can be responsible for planning, designing and evaluating efforts to achieve healthy nutrition.

Community advisory committee

It is also important to work with groups and individuals outside of the school who have an impact on students' knowledge, attitudes and behaviours related to eating. If the school or school district has a community advisory committee, it is essential to find out whether they address health promotion and nutrition. If such a committee does not exist, implementing healthy nutrition provides an opportunity to form one or to identify community advisors who can work with the school health team to improve health and nutrition. In some settings it may be beneficial to collaborate with existing community groups, such as a healthy city council or school board.

Potential partners from outside the school include: representatives of local government, community residents, businesses, vendors, media, community youth agencies, nongovernmental organizations, social service providers, health service providers, sports figures and religious leaders. Subsequently, this committee can also address other health promotion issues. To facilitate the efforts of the school health team, the community advisory committee, or selected advisors, can help determine local needs and resources, disseminate information about health and healthy nutrition, build support across the community, encourage community involvement, help to obtain resources and funding for health and nutrition interventions, and reinforce learning experiences provided in school.

The committee should include men and women with a diversity of skills who are influential in the community or district, interested in health promotion and healthy nutrition, able to mobilize support and connections, and represent the community's geographical areas as well as economic, social, ethnic and religious makeup. The community advisory committee and the school health team should work together in planning health promotion efforts and in coordinating the various components of a Health-Promoting School, such as health education, health services, community and family involvement, etc., so that all aspects of health promotion work together for health and healthy nutrition.

Situation Analysis

A situation analysis should be considered by policy- and decision-makers and other interested groups at national, district and local levels to support the development of a Health-Promoting School and healthy nutrition. At the local level, once a school health team and community advisory committee or other responsible authorities are established, they can start planning interventions by conducting a situation analysis. Conducting a situation analysis will help people to better understand the needs, resources and conditions that are relevant to planning interventions. The necessity for an adequate situation analysis on a national, district and/or local school level is justified by several reasons:

— Policy- and decision-makers will need a strong basis for their support, especially when their policies and decisions involve the allocation of resources.

— Accurate and up-to-date data and information provide a basis for discussion, justification, setting priorities for action and identifying groups in special need for intervention, such as children belonging to underprivileged and minority groups or living in geographical areas where nutritional deficiencies are prevalent.

— Data obtained through the situation analysis are essential for planning and evaluating interventions. Data can help ensure that programmes focus on the actual health needs, experience, motivation and strengths of the target population so that interventions increase physical, social and mental well-being of students, staff, families and community members. Data also serve as a baseline to observe future trends in nutritional status and dietary behaviour.

Information needed

Various quantitative and qualitative information is needed for planning health promotion and nutrition interventions and for establishing a baseline for evaluation. Quantitative information includes numbers and scores while qualitative information includes perceptions and feelings.

The following information can help determine local needs concerning nutrition:

— Current health and nutritional status at national, regional, local and/or school level and how well it corresponds with relevant guidelines. This data should include the proportion of persons who are affected by malnutrition and infections and how severely they are affected.

— Knowledge, attitudes, beliefs, values, behaviours and conditions related to health and nutrition, eating patterns and food customs. For example, people might not know which foods are nutritious; poorly prepared food may influence a student's attitude about food that may be highly nutritious; local beliefs or superstitions may prevent people from eating certain foods; people might choose to ignore conditions of malnutrition because they have been with them for generations; or people might not be familiar with precautions to safely preserve food. This information is crucial to design effective health promotion strategies because values, beliefs and attitudes positively or negatively influence behaviours and conditions associated with nutrition and health. Without information about these helping or hindering forces, educational interventions are not likely to be targeted to the most relevant factors that contribute to health or malnutrition in the community and thus are unlikely to achieve the desired result.

— Available resources in the school and community. This includes determining which specific personnel and financial resources and services are available. Assessments should include the nature and extent of existing programmes, either through the school or community, that might help in implementing health promotion and nutrition interventions, such as deworming, oral hygiene or sport programmes. Knowing this information allows the school health team to draw on available resources for implementing new programmes or improving existing ones. It is not all inclusive, as close collaboration between education and health officials, schools and community members is essential in assessing each particular nation, district or local school/community.

Data sources

In obtaining the above information it is important to collaborate with health, education and agriculture authorities; community organizations; mass media; teachers; parents; students and others to share available data sources and to avoid duplication of assessments. Data about nutritional status and levels of malnutrition may be available from the local health unit or from other local or regional organizations. Youth risk behaviour surveys or other health-related assessments could provide valuable information that can be integrated into the situation analysis.

Data from existing reports and surveys should be carefully reviewed before deciding on the necessity to undertake a new survey of current needs. Where data is not available, simple and well-tried assessment tools should be used to identify relevant conditions and behaviours. For instance, food frequency questionnaires can assist students and others to estimate how frequently certain foods are usually consumed. This information can then be compared with established guidelines. To reduce unnecessary repetitions of such assessments in schools, the collection of nutrition-related knowledge, behaviours and conditions may be most efficiently done as part of a broad survey of health-related behaviours and conditions.

Nutrition interventions in a Health-Promoting School are most successful when a wide range of individuals and groups support the programme and become involved in it. It is important in the early stages to secure the acceptance and support of government officials, community and business leaders, educators, parents, students and the community in general.

National policies, guidelines and support from ministries of health, education, food and agriculture can be of immense help to local schools. Efforts to promote healthy nutrition through schools are most successful with the will, commitment, attention, support and action of these authorities. Collaborative relationships with other sectors and with local governments will also prove valuable. Political commitment is evidenced by:

— Public acknowledgement by government officials of the importance of nutrition for health, education and development and the importance of providing nutrition interventions.
— Clear sanction and support from the ministries of education, health, food and agriculture for health promotion and nutrition interventions.
— Designation of someone with responsibility and authority at national, district and local levels to deal with health and nutrition issues and pian interventions.
— Financial support for school health promotion and nutrition interventions.
— Training, equipment and materials to enable schools to develop and implement health and nutrition interventions.

Community commitment

The success of efforts to create a Health-Promoting School relies also on the extent to which people in the community are aware of and willing to support health promotion efforts. Schools need to receive input from parents and community members regarding the design, delivery, content and assessment of school health promotion, so as to respond to their concerns and to attain their commitment. Family and community members should be involved very early; for instance, through community group meetings, parent-teacher associations, formal presentations, open houses, civic clubs and religious centres. Commitment and support of many parties on various levels is needed to share expertise, facilities and resources.

Partnerships of representative individuals, groups and organizations from numerous sectors, such as nongovernment, education, health, business, agriculture, communication, recreation, voluntary service and religion can demonstrate and provide commitment, resources and support for health promotion and nutrition interventions. Community commitment is strengthened/marked by:

— Public acknowledgement of the importance of healthy nutrition by community leaders and local health, education, agricultural and other relevant organizations and businesses.

— Establishment of a designated committee for coordinating community nutrition interventions.

— Provision of local resources for health and nutrition interventions in schools.

— Coordination of interventions with other programmes in the community (e.g. food supplementation programmes, farmers' support programmes, food safety efforts).

— Efforts to attract community and media attention (e.g. through printed material, community forums, tours of places that produce or process food).

Supportive school policies

Supportive school policies provide an essential framework that guides schools in planning, implementing and evaluating efforts to promote health and healthy nutrition. School policies are brief documents that promote a clear set of school norms regarding health and nutrition. They incorporate input from all relevant constituents of the school community: students, teachers, parents, staff, administrators, food service personnel, nurses and counsellors. Policies need to meet national and local needs and standards and should be adapted to the health concerns, food preferences and dietary practices of different ethnic and cultural groups represented at school.

Policies that support collaboration and coordination between the health, education, food and agricultural sectors of the government and between the school and the community are encouraged. Written policies should guarantee nutrition and other health interventions for all levels of schooling, starting in the earliest grade and continuing through the last grade. Policies should address all components of a Health-Promoting School that will be modified, such as education about nutrition, food choices at the school canteen, feeding programmes, family involvement and food handling procedures.

Especially important are regulations about a Health-Promoting School's environment and about health education. For instance, school policies should guarantee adequate sanitation, a pleasant eating environment and collaboration with vendors as well as provision of teacher training, learning materials and a curriculum for nutrition and health education. Specific examples of supportive school policies include: Regulations, rules and protocols that ensure:

— students, parents, teachers and other school personnel are involved in planning of health promotion and nutrition interventions; for instance, through their participation on the school health team.

— the community advisory committee meets periodically to sustain coordination between school and community.

– the school curriculum includes education about nutrition as part of a sequential, comprehensive school health education programme, as an integral part of other relevant subject areas or, ideally, as a combination of both.

- teachers and other school personnel receive ongoing training about nutrition and food safety.
- all school facilities and events, including cafeterias, snack bars, rewards, staff meetings, parents' meetings and special events serve nutritious food, based on local, district and/or national guidelines
- parents are educated about the value of healthy meals and food safety practices and about their role as reinforcers and motivators of concepts and knowledge for better eating and learning.
- school health services offer screening for conditions of malnutrition among students (where relevant) and report the results to teachers, parents and community members.

Goals and Objectives of Nutrition Interventions in Schools

Using the information gathered in the situation analysis, the school health team, in collaboration with the community advisory committee, can develop a vision for change and an action plan. This provides a basis for formulating goals and objectives for health promotion and nutrition interventions. Goals and objectives are necessary to make clear what the interventions should achieve. They are also essential to evaluate the extent to which the desired outcomes have been reached.

The goals should describe in broad terms what the programme will achieve. Nutrition intervention goals of a Health-Promoting School should aim at:

- gaining the full health and educational potential of food and nutrition sources for students and other members of the school, family and community.
- applying the school's full organizational potential to improve the nutritional status of students, staff, families and community members.
- laying a foundation of lifelong healthy eating based on favourable experiences, sufficient skills and confidence in one's capacity to practice a healthy lifestyle.

The goals are then broken down into specific outcome and process objectives so that everyone clearly understands what needs to be done, when and why. Objectives are steps for reaching the overall goal and describe outcomes in measurable terms that will help determine how successfully the goal is being reached.

Outcome objectives are established to define in measurable terms what is to be achieved through the interventions regarding health status of participants; and changes in knowledge, attitudes, beliefs, behaviours and conditions related to health and nutrition status. Thus, they help define and determine the success of the school-based nutrition interventions. Examples of outcome objectives:

— measurable health indicators related to nutrition (e.g. weight-for-height scores, blood iron levels, blood cholesterol levels) will have reached at least (value) for at least ..% of students/parents/teachers.

— knowledge, attitudes and behaviour that are relevant to students' and parents' nutrition (e.g. knowledge of dietary guidelines; attitudes about the importance of diet to health and well-being; behaviour related to food consumption) will have increased .. % over baseline.

— the percentage of (students/teachers/parents) that can demonstrate at least two methods of ensuring food safety, as given in the WHO Golden Rules for Safe Food Preparation, will be increased to at least .. %.

Process objectives describe what will be changed or implemented to achieve the outcome objectives. Examples of process objectives:

— the number of Health-Promoting Schools in the (district/nation) which have implemented nutrition interventions will have increased from (number) to (number).

— at least (number) of the following interventions will be implemented to make the school environment more health-enhancing

— healthy meal choices are provided in the school cafeteria routine messages are sent to parents about low cost healthy lunches that can be prepared for their children

— posters that reinforce social norms related to healthy eating, such as eating with a friend, taking time to eat, etc., are displayed

— school health services include screening for nutritional deficiencies.

— at least (number) of the following interventions will be implemented to enhance nutrition-related school health education:

— nutrition-related learning experiences are integrated into a course of instruction in each successive grade level

— training for teachers and other school staff on health promotion and nutrition education is held at least once per (year/semester)

— a series of extra-curricular workshops for students, staff and parents are conducted on preparing specific healthy and safe meals and completing dietary self-assessment.

— at least ... % of (students/parents/teachers) will have implemented or participated in (number) of the following interventions to enhance healthy nutrition:

— providing education about nutrition in a relevant subject area

— organizing or contributing to nutrition-related school/community project

— screening for indicators of conditions of malnutrition

— creating an environment that enhances health and healthy nutrition.

Various Components of Health-Promoting School

A Health-Promoting School strives to use the school's full organizational capacity to improve the health of students, school personnel, families and community members. Such a school offers many opportunities to promote nutrition as an essential element for the attainment of health. Nutrition interventions can serve as an entry point for the development or enhancement of policies, planning groups and various components which serve as a framework for a Health-Promoting School. These components include, but are not limited to :

—School health education	Community and family involvement and outreach
—Healthy school environment	Physical exercise, recreation and sport
—School health services	Counselling and social support
—Nutrition and food programmes -	Health promotion for school staff

The effectiveness of interventions integrated into each of the above components is influenced by the extent to which they are supported by a variety of people, policies and trained staff. The effectiveness is also influenced by the extent to which interventions in each of these components combine with other health promotion efforts to complement and reinforce each other. Not all schools will have the resources to integrate nutrition interventions into all of the components at one time. Therefore, each school has to establish its own priorities, in collaboration with all parties concerned, to decide the extent to which the components should be addressed.

A Health-Promoting School enables students, parents, teachers and community members to work together to make such decisions. It is more important to start with small changes that are possible than to wait until resources become available to address all of these components simultaneously.

School Health Education

The primary goals of school health education are to help individuals adopt behaviours and to create conditions that are conducive to health. Thus, the clear and precise delineation of behaviours and conditions specifically relevant to healthy nutrition is essential for the development of effective school health education efforts. These are not all inclusive, and national guidelines are available that provide advice relevant to individuals in specific countries. Close collaboration between education, health and food officials; the school health team; the community advisory committee; and other school and community members is necessary to identify the nutrition-related behaviours and conditions relevant to health in each community.

School health education is designed to help students acquire the knowledge, attitudes, beliefs and skills which are needed to make informed decisions, practice healthy behaviours and create conditions that are conducive to health.

— Knowledge provides a factual background on which to base decisions, such as knowledge about the relationship of eating and health and about planning for healthy nutrition using assessments and nutritional guidelines.

— Attitudes provide a personal perception for decisions, such as feeling responsible for one's own health and the health of others.

— Beliefs provide a conviction for decisions, such as a belief that healthy eating makes a positive difference in well-being.

— Skills provide a practical basis for mastering tasks and procedures related to healthy eating, such as skills for selecting and preparing healthy meals and practising food safety.

In a Health-Promoting School, school health education about nutrition addresses food, its preparation and its consumption as an essential positive and enjoyable aspect of life. A Health-Promoting School provides opportunities for students to practice important skills, such as decision-making about food choices. To be relevant to student needs, learning experiences should be related to food preferences and other motivational factors that guide students to improve their nutrition and that of their family and community. School health education about nutrition should also teach that lifestyle influences a person's food requirements.

In a Health-Promoting School, curricula are also designed to address the emotional and sociocultural aspects of healthy eating along with informational and skill-building learning experiences. They may be helpful to people who are responsible for identifying the knowledge, attitudes, beliefs and skills that are most relevant to health in their own communities. School health education should be provided as a planned sequential course of instruction from the primary through the secondary levels, addressing the physical, mental, emotional and social dimensions of health. It can be taught as a specific subject, as part of other subjects, or ideally, as a combination of both. Thus, health education about nutrition should be an important part of a school health curriculum; integrated into such subject areas as science, home economics, mathematics, and agriculture; as well as included in the school's extracurricular activities.

Nutrition education will enhance the overall framework of a Health-Promoting School if it is integrated into other school health components, such as physical activity and health promotion for staff, as well as in the school health education component. Education about nutrition should be combined with efforts addressing other health issues, such as reproductive health, life skills, and alcohol and drug use prevention, so that the learning experiences will complement and reinforce each other. Linking these issues can be accomplished by organizing them into a school health education curriculum and coordinating the simultaneous or sequential presentation of related topics in different classes. Health promotion for school

Linkages of health and nutrition issues and other relevant topics can also be facilitated by co-teaching, sharing teaching resources, referring students to related lessons and involving students from different classes in group activities. Curricula for nutrition and other health-related issues may be available through governmental and nongovernmental agencies and organizations, universities or teachers' unions. Supplemental materials specific to the local situation can also be generated by teachers and students themselves.

Educational methods such as lectures, discussions, debates, role-plays and audio-visual aids should be designed or selected to increase knowledge, build positive attitudes and values, dispel myths, increase skills and provide support for the development of healthy lifestyles. They need to be appropriate for the developmental level of students. The selection of an educational method should be based on the extent to which that method is appropriate to influence the factors, such as knowledge, attitudes, skills, etc., associated with nutrition-related behaviours and conditions that contribute to health and to the prevention of malnutrition. For example, a lecture is an effective way to increase knowledge but is less effective in influencing beliefs and building skills.

Discussions, debates and carefully prepared written materials can be more effective than a lecture in dispelling local myths. Practice sessions, such as cooking nutritious recipes and growing food in a school garden, can be more effective than lectures, discussions, debates and written materials in building skills. These are not all inclusive. A diversity of instructional strategies is essential to effective curriculum development. In selecting information to convey to students about nutrition, scientific terms and details are considered less important than practical and basic information that will enable students to make healthy food choices and to prepare foods safely. For example, it is more essential for a student to know how to prepare a healthy meal than to learn the exact grams of nutrients in different foods.

Students are more likely to adopt healthy eating patterns when they learn about these behaviours through enjoyable and participatory activities that emphasize the positive aspects of healthy eating in a context of what is relevant and important to students. Students should have repeated opportunities to taste and choose a variety of foods with high nutritional value. They should have learning opportunities to acquire knowledge, attitudes and skills that they can apply in school, at home and in the community. An action-oriented learning process should also help students recognise the importance of socialization during meal times and of making appropriate choices and decisions about health and nutrition.

The types of selected activities will depend upon whether their purpose is to:

— Inform - to provide information that can be understood by the students in a way that is useful

— Motivate - to help inspire and sustain interest in developing, continuing or changing health-promoting activities or behaviours

— Enable/facilitate - to provide tools, mechanisms, skills or other means by which the students can perform healthy behaviours

— Reinforce - to support the continuation of a desired behaviour, activity or change process.

Training teachers to implement health education

Teacher training, both pre-service and in-service, is an important factor in a successful school health education programme. Teacher training should sensitise them to the concept of health promotion in schools. All teachers need to receive training and accurate information to effectively address health and nutrition in their content area. Education and training should inspire and equip teachers with knowledge and skills to make a curriculum exciting in order to encourage students to build healthy eating practices and to make nutritious food choices. In addition, training should help teachers assess and improve their own eating practices and make them aware of behavioural messages they give as role models.

Teachers who are primarily responsible for nutrition education should receive specific and relevant training in implementing a selected curriculum. This training should address content and teaching strategies. Since nutrition education involves influencing attitudes, beliefs and skills, as well as knowledge to promote healthy behaviours and conditions, teachers must be trained to use a wide variety of teaching methods.

Ideally, training should be ongoing and provide time for sharing strategies. It should involve monitoring performance and evaluating health and nutrition programmes. Team training of teachers can help assure consistent application of health promotion and nutrition interventions in different classrooms and throughout the school. Training and learning materials for teacher training may be available through governmental and nongovernmental agencies and organizations, universities or teachers' unions. Supplemental training materials specific to the local situation can also be generated by teachers and students themselves.

Healthy School Environment

The school's environment plays a significant role in determining whether interventions to promote health and healthy nutrition will be effective and sustainable. Thus, students should have access to food of high nutritional value and to the support of persons around them to develop and maintain a healthy diet. A Health-Promoting School provides a safe and healthy environment that presents a realistic and attractive range of health choices to encourage a healthy lifestyle. It also helps students and others develop their physical, psychological and social potential. In a Health-Promoting School, the physical and psychosocial school environment should be consistent with and reinforce other health promotion efforts .

Physical environment

The physical environment includes the school building, classrooms, eating facilities, water and foods provided at school and the surroundings in which the school is situated. The condition of the physical environment can have a powerful effect on reinforcing or contradicting health education and nutrition interventions in the school. The following nutrition-related aspects of a healthy physical environment can be integrated into a Health-Promoting School, supported by related school health policies:

— *Sanitation:* In schools, the presence of clean water, safe food and sanitary facilities as well as proper waste collection and disposal are essential to good health and nutrition. Adequate sanitation contributes to reducing the risk for food-borne and other infections related to health and nutrition.

— *Healthy food choices:* A Health-Promoting School promotes and provides appropriate healthy and high quality foods and meals to offer opportunities for healthy choices.

— *Pleasant eating environment*: A pleasant eating environment in a Health-Promoting School provides sufficient space and comfortable surroundings for socializing during meal times and for enjoyment of food, which in turn enhance mental, social and physical health.

— *Outside vendors:* Efforts to create a health-conducive environment should also include food vendors that may be present on or near the school property, who provide an important source of food for students. Schools should strive to gain cooperation with vendors to offer nutritious food choices to encourage the school's health promotion efforts.

— *Special facilities:* A Health-Promoting School may also have facilities to carry out practical nutrition-related activities, such as food preparation, food experiments and growing food.

For creating a healthy physical school environment, food services and food safety are key factors that must be addressed.

School food services

School food services need to be integrated into and coordinated with health and nutrition education and with other components of the Health-Promoting School to reinforce messages on healthy eating and ensure consistent nutrition support. The school cafeteria provides a place for students to practice healthy eating. Therefore, the school canteen needs to offer a variety of healthy food choices and limit the availability of food with low nutritional value to help students apply skills taught in the classroom.

The food supply at the school canteen should be based on national or regional dietary guidelines if these are applicable to children. Local stores, businesses or farmers can be involved in providing nutritious food and/or food from school gardens could be used to keep costs low and to collaborate with different sectors in the community.

In addition to offering nutritious food choices, food service personnel can also be involved in other components of a Health-Promoting School. Some examples of how the activities of food service personnel can contribute to the development of a Health-Promoting School include:

— visiting classrooms and explaining how they make sure meals meet the standards of the dietary guidelines

— inviting classes to visit the cafeteria kitchen and learn how to prepare healthy meals

— involving students in planning the school menu and preparing recipes

— offering foods that reinforce classroom lessons (e.g. whole wheat bread to reinforce a lesson on dietary fibre)

— posting in the cafeteria, or where children eat, information and guidance about nutrition and its value to health

— displaying nutrition information about available foods

— giving students opportunities to practice food analysis and selection skills learned in the classroom.

Food safety

It is important that environmental conditions in schools ensure a safe food supply. Such conditions are supported by clean and safe water and food, safe means of waste disposal, good standards of hygiene, cleanliness, tidiness and adequate ventilation. These efforts should be reinforced through personnel at school. Applying rules for safe food preparation is also essential for students, teachers and service providers.

Environmental efforts to ensure food safety should support instructional content on the same subject. While each school should follow the regulations and standards established by their respective government concerning food safety, WHO has developed the following general Golden Rules for Safe Food Preparation:

1. Choose foods processed for safety.
2. Cook food thoroughly.
3. Eat cooked foods immediately.
4. Store cooked foods carefully.
5. Reheat cooked foods thoroughly.
6. Avoid contact between raw foods and cooked foods.
7. Wash hands repeatedly with soap and water.

8. Keep all kitchen surfaces meticulously clean.
9. Protect foods from insects, rodents and other animals.
10. Use safe water.

Psychosocial environment

The psychosocial environment relates to social and mental conditions which affect education and health. This incorporates the cultural norms and expectations regarding food and eating patterns as expressed by friends, parents and school personnel. A Health-Promoting School provides an ambience which respects the individual and fosters confidence in healthy choices and enjoyment of food. The following aspects of a healthy psychosocial environment should be integrated into a Health-Promoting School:

— *Support:* The psychosocial environment should support health-conducive perceptions and actions of all who live, work and learn in the school. It should be consistent with other health-promoting interventions in the school and classroom. For instance, the friendliness and support of school staff as well as community members involved in school projects can contribute to psychosocial support. Such support can help build confidence and self-esteem with regard to healthy eating practices.

— *Teacher role models:* One aspect of the school's psychosocial environment is the important role that teachers play as adult role models and as mentors. For instance, teachers can encourage students to follow a healthy way of life by demonstrating healthy eating.

— *Peer reinforcement:* Another aspect is students' influence on peers. Students can provide positive reinforcement to their peers by advising and reminding each other of healthy eating habits. This requires that schools provide students with sufficient time to eat and socialize.

School Health Services

School health services help to prevent, reduce, monitor or treat important health problems or conditions as well as foster health and well-being. In a Health-Promoting School, health services work in partnership with and are provided for students, school personnel, families and community members. They should be coordinated with other services and activities at school and in the community to utilise the potential of specialist resources to provide advice and support for health promotion and nutrition interventions. Schools and communities need to consider what preventive and treatment services are best provided at school sites and avoid duplicating services available in the community that would easily be accessible for students and school personnel.

Models for providing school health services vary tremendously, not only from developed to developing countries but also among and within nations themselves. School health services can consist of a teacher designated to be responsible for first aid, a trained school nurse or a school health team. Such staff contribute to the well-being of students, faculty and community through caring for individuals' health and nutritional status.

Their roles can include screening for indicators of malnutrition and health status, providing treatments such as micronutrient supplements and parasite medications, referring to appropriate nutritional and other services, and supplying health and nutrition information to teachers and students to help them make healthy decisions and to educate others about healthy nutrition. Institutions of higher education that train medical professionals and paraprofessionals or nongovernmental organizations may provide training for school health service providers.

Although not all schools can provide access to school health services, where resources are available, the following nutrition-related services should be considered:

Screening/Diagnosis

Screening and diagnosis of health and nutritional status, including conditions of malnutrition, can play an important role in planning efforts to enhance health or influence unhealthy eating habits. Nutritional screening can include food consumption surveys, which are compared to food guidelines, as well as measurements of body weight and height, which are compared to a subject's age and sex. In addition, blood tests can be used to diagnose micronutrient deficiencies, such as iron deficiency anaemia and indicators of nutrition-related chronic diseases, such as high blood cholesterol.

Referral

Based on the results of screening, the school health services can provide contact and referrals to other school services, such as feeding programmes or counselling services, and, as appropriate, to local health services and other community agencies which can respond to the identified needs. School health services can also provide information about where to obtain nutritious food, dietary guidelines and other appropriate services.

Nutrition and Food Programmes

Children who are not adequately nourished are more likely to be absent from school, less likely to concentrate and perform well and more likely to be susceptible to infections. Therefore, a Health-Promoting School should integrate efforts to ensure students' nutritional adequacy into a variety of its health promotion interventions. Where needed, the school can provide nutritious meals or micronutrient supplements that help relieve some of these problems.

Feeding programmes

School feeding programmes are one example of interventions aiming at increasing food availability while promoting healthy eating. These programmes might provide breakfast, lunch and/or snacks at reduced price or free of charge, providing calories, protein and micronutrients to schoolchildren without adequate food. Feeding programmes have been shown to increase weight and in some cases also school attendance and achievement. The composition of provided meals in terms of food items and nutritional value has been shown to play a role in educational achievement. For instance, research with elementary and high school students in Chile showed improvements in educational accomplishments with more frequent consumption of dairy products and with more nutrient intake, in particular protein and calcium.

Micronutrient supplementation

Diets deficient in essential vitamins and minerals can have an enormous health impact. Thus, micronutrient supplementation is another example of nutrition interventions to prevent specific deficiency diseases in individuals and to promote well-being. This intervention method supplies micronutrients separately from the normal diet. Children who receive supplements must obtain them regularly; therefore, schools are an appropriate place to distribute them. Micronutrient supplements can be given orally or by injection. These supplements may include vitamin A capsules to prevent blindness, iron tablets to prevent anaemia and iodized oil or iodized salt to prevent goitre and mental retardation. Ample evidence exists of the value of treating micronutrient deficiencies resulting in improved performance at school or work and reduced burden of illness, disability and death.

Community and Family Involvement and Outreach

A Health-Promoting School provides a setting which addresses health promotion and healthy nutrition by engaging students, school personnel, families and community members in collaborative and integrated efforts to improve health in the school and through school/community projects and outreach. Family and community members can be involved in Health-Promoting Schools in various ways:

— Taking part in planning and decision-making; for instance, participating in the school health team or community advisory committee.

— Participating in activities and services offered through schools; for instance, attending projects to gain specific health and nutritional knowledge and skills, such as in exhibitions, photo expositions, concerts, drama, community-wide entertainment, festivals and health fairs.

— Providing support and resources; for instance, supplying financial or material donations, being guest speakers or providing specialist services related to health and nutrition. Nutritionists from the community can offer nutritional assessments for students and parents, and supermarkets and farms can offer healthy food.

— Advocating for health; for instance, knowledge and skills acquired in a school/community project can be used by community and family members to take communal actions that will result in sustainable healthy eating practices.

The family and community also provide a setting for students to understand, practice and share what they learn about health and nutrition in the classroom. They have the potential to support and reinforce nutrition education and health promotion. Thus, it is essential that school staff, parents and community members work together in order to create conditions that allow the maximum attainment of health by all its members. Students are most likely to adopt healthy eating patterns if they receive consistent information and support through multiple channels, such as parents, peers, teachers, community members and media. Thus, a Health-Promoting School should strengthen community links and involve parents and the wider community as much as possible. Community members and parents, in turn, should feel that their school is open and receptive to their ideas and participation.

Outreach to community and family members is especially important in places where a high percentage of young people do not attend school since community outreach from schools has the potential to reach those who are not reached by schools directly. Everybody should have the opportunity to take responsibility for decisions conducive to health for themselves and others whom they care for.

Collaboration with parents and families

Health-Promoting Schools should closely collaborate with parents so that children are less likely to experience inconsistencies between suggestions and practices at home and at school. Thus, establishing dynamic, positive and productive links with families is an important part of a Health-Promoting School. Connections with parents can be established, for instance, during a school health fair to which parents are invited, a healthrelated workshop for parents, a parent-teacher meeting or a parent's visit to relevant food services at school or in the community. Parents and other caregivers play an important role in their child's life in their roles as nurturer, teacher, disciplinarian, role model and supervisor since parents control most of the food choices available at home. Therefore, it is essential that they understand and reinforce what the Health-Promoting School seeks to achieve.

The school can provide parents and family members with information, resources and skills about important principles of healthy nutrition in an effort to enhance and extend the programme in the student's home. Improving parents' eating habits may be one of the most effective ways to promote healthy eating for their children as parents create conditions at home that are conducive or not conducive to healthy nutrition. At the elementary school level, involving parents in nutrition-related learning experiences such as games, take-home activities and meals in school, is especially effective in enhancing the eating behaviours of both the students and the parents. Thus, parent involvement should begin early. In addition to learning about healthy eating, parents can also contribute services or resources to the school and participate in or lead community efforts that promote health and healthy nutrition.

Collaboration with the community

Cooperation and coordination between the school health programme and the community is likely to be most successful where there are dynamic, positive and productive school/community links. Schools and communities can benefit from partnerships with local businesses and representatives from agencies and organizations, such as local health departments, farmers' organizations, youth-serving agencies and local retailers. For instance, the school can utilise the potential of specialist services in the community for advice and support in nutrition and health matters and can actively involve community nutritionists and community health services at school.

Commercial organisations and businesses can offer health-related and relevant visits to their stores, advice on healthy choices or donations in support of nutrition programmes. Subsequently, they may gain customers and recognition for their efforts in support of health. Constructive collaboration is especially important with national and local food businesses, supermarkets, restaurants and food vendors in an effort to gain their support for healthy nutrition and to involve them in supplying food with high nutritional value. Partnerships may involve communication among organisations and schools, cooperation of jointly scheduled activities, coordination of resources and collaboration under a mutually agreed mission.

Involving mass media

Mass media can encourage new behaviours. They can be used on a national and local scale as well as in classrooms for health promotion and nutrition interventions. Mass media include radio, television, signboards, posters, calendars, comics, photo novels, newspapers, magazines, booklets, leaflets, audiovisual materials and traditional communication forms such as dance troupes. For instance, nutritional radio, television quiz programmes for schoolchildren and crossword puzzles in children's newspapers have been utilised to promote health and nutrition. Some materials can be distributed through more than one channel or can be used with different target groups: a nutrition teacher with a cassette recorder can play the same programme at the village well that can be broadcast over radio or discussed in class.

Multimedia approaches that combine face-to-face and mass channels are appropriate for nutrition education because nutrition is relevant to everyone and different channels are necessary for different phases in the learning process. Food advertising is also a pervasive and influential aspect of the media. Children have to be taught to recognize the purposes of advertising strategies such as those which provide important information and those solely promoting a particular product. Children also need to learn to recognize that some advertising may not be supportive of good nutrition.

If advertising sources are involved in school/community efforts, they can also be helpful in informing people about facts of good nutrition. It is important that materials targeted towards children with dietary information and advice are consistent with official health standards and guidelines. They could be launched by various partners in the nutrition field: government agencies, industry and trade, consumer organisations, insurance companies, sport organisations, municipalities, etc. School and health representatives should be included in the planning teams for such materials and offer their special skills and experiences.

Physical Exercise, Recreation and Sport

Eating a healthy diet does not in itself guarantee good health. A healthy diet is however an important part of a healthy lifestyle that also includes physical exercise, not using tobacco in any form, not drinking alcoholic beverages in excess and not abusing drugs. All of these issues should thus be addressed by a Health-Promoting School in an organized and complementary manner.

The importance of addressing lifestyle holistically is clearly illustrated in the linkage between nutrition and active living. Physical exercise, recreation and sport help individuals acquire and maintain physical fitness and serve as a healthy means of self-expression and social development. Expending energy in physical exercise and sport balances the intake of energy from food, especially in regions that do not incorporate physical activity into daily living through farming, herding animals, walking long distances or other activities. Thus, physical activity and nutrition must be addressed in a complementary manner when integrated into the components of a Health- Promoting School.

Nutrition interventions should stress that all children and adults should have the opportunity to attain the healthful benefits of exercise, games, dance, sport or an active lifestyle. In regions where overnutrition is prevalent, efforts to promote physical activity and sport should stress the benefits of reducing the risk of obesity and related disorders since negative health consequences of overweight and obesity are likely to be more serious in sedentary than in active obese people. Thus, physical exercise and sport, together with healthy nutrition, can help reduce the effects of age and chronic disease on heart, lungs and muscles; reduce fatigue, mild anxiety and depression; and diminish the loss of bone calcium while creating vigour, stamina and other fundamental requirements for well-being.

Additionally, recreation activities and healthy nutrition can restore strength and spirits after school and work. Ball games, dances or other recreational events can be supportive of good health and offer nutritious food. In a Health-Promoting School, personnel, community members and families can participate together in planning and implementing such activities which in turn strengthen community spirit.

Counselling and Social Support

Maintaining and supporting the mental health of students and staff should also be addressed in a Health-Promoting School in a manner which complements and supports nutritional and physical health. An individual's psychological well-being, including self-esteem and self-confidence, is critical in maintaining physical health and the ability to make healthy decisions and avoid risk behaviours. Thus, school counselling programmes and actions to provide social support are important components of a Health-Promoting School that can help students, school personnel and families in coping with difficulties, adjustments, growth and development.

Personal feelings and emotions influence food choices. For example, one's body image or low self-esteem can affect eating practices and lead to conditions of malnutrition. Achieving and maintaining desired body weight and shape can be very important for young people, especially for girls, and may lead to dieting, meal skipping and nutritional disorders.

Consequently, counselling services or actions to provide social support can be provided by a Health-Promoting School or should be addressed through referral to a community service. This will help adolescents clarify misconceptions about their self-perception, which is a prerequisite to developing a healthy self-image and adopting a healthy lifestyle and good eating habits.

For children and adults to thrive they not only need an appropriate diet and body image but also care and nurturing. Care is the provision of time, attention, support and skills that can help meet individuals' physical, mental and social needs. A supportive psychosocial environment within the school can provide a buffering effect on transitions or stressful life events experienced by students and others. For instance, social and emotional support can be provided during meals by any member of the school community for individuals who are changing their eating behaviour. Social support can also strengthen students to resist social pressures to eat food of low nutritional value since eating is influenced by social forces (6). Thus, care and support services can enhance nutrition interventions by encouraging students and others to make appropriate choices about their diet, promoting self-esteem and supporting students' efforts to fulfill their physical, psychological and social potential.

Health Promotion for School Staff

A Health-Promoting School aims at promoting healthy lifestyles among all who study, work anduse the school. Thus, strategies to promote health and nutrition should become an integral partof a Health-Promoting School; for instance, as part of in-service training. School health promotionprogrammes for staff are intended to increase their interest in health and help them acquirehealthy lifestyles. Examples for nutritional health promotion include printed materials from nationalor local organizations, healthy meals and guidelines provided by the school cafeteria, and workshops for staff members held by community nutritionists or others.

There are several reasons why health promotion for school personnel is important. First, healthyemployees are better able to fulfill their responsibilities. Thus, health promotion activities shouldhelp them assess and improve their own eating practices. Second, teachers and schoolpersonnel need to be aware of and responsible for the messages they give as role models tostudents and others. Third, school personnel can help identify policies and practices thatare needed in order to support health and well-being in a Health-Promoting School. A healthpromotion programme for staff can help develop those policies that support their health and findways to change those policies that are not conducive to the health of teachers and other staff.

Evaluation

Evaluation is a powerful tool that can be used to inform about and to strengthen school healthprogrammes. The primary intentions of most evaluations are to provide information about theextent to which the programme is being implemented as planned and having the intended effect.Evaluation helps to:

— Provide information to policy-makers, sponsors, planners, administrators and participants about the implementation and effect of the programme.

— Provide feedback to those involved in project planning to determine which parts of the programme are working well and which are not.

— Make improvements or adjustments in the process of implementation.

— Value the effort of schools, parents and communities.

— Document experience gained from the project so that it can be shared with others.

Responsible officials, such as members of the school health team or their designees, should regularly review the implementation process and the effectiveness of school health interventions. All groups affected by the programme should have the opportunity to provide input. Based upon the results of information gathered from evaluation, those involved in planning and implementing the interventions will make decisions concerning the programme and its various components.

Types of Evaluation

There are two main types of evaluation which are most relevant to evaluating school health programmes: process and outcome evaluation.

Process evaluation

This type of evaluation assesses how well the interventions are being implemented. Process evaluation should be ongoing to determine what interventions have actually been delivered, to whom and when. This will help to assess progress toward the programme's goals and objectives. Evaluation of the planning, development and implementation processes of the programme provides information on which mid-course adjustments can be made and documentation for others who want to learn from the implementation process. Methods for process evaluation involve tallies, record keeping by schools and interviews with teachers, school administrators and others.

Process evaluation answers questions such as:

— To what extent are the interventions being implemented the way they are intended?

— To what extent are the interventions reaching the individuals who may need them (e.g. students, parents, teachers, community members)?

Outcome evaluation

Outcome evaluation measures whether and to what extent outcome objectives have been achieved. It is concerned with the effect of the interventions and helps to determine whether any changes have occurred following the implementation of a programme. If the traditional pre- and post-test design is used, quantitative and qualitative indicators of nutrition-related health status, behaviours, knowledge, attitudes and/or beliefs will be compared before and after the implementation of the interventions. Thus, data items collected during the needs assessment can be of significant value to the outcome evaluation process.

Quantitative data include objective numerical measures, such as weight-for-height-scores, prevalence of healthy behaviour and of malnutrition conditions. Qualitative data contain subjective perceptions and feelings, such as feeling in control of one's food choices and satisfaction about one's nutritional health status. Outcome evaluation can demonstrate the benefits of school health promotion programmes or further need for such programmes. Evaluation results can be brought to the attention of the community and can be used to convince others to get involved in the programme.

Any evaluation is useful and complete only when its results are reported and communicated tothose who need them and can use them. The value of evaluations is increased if the results arereported using repeatedly the same objective criteria to ensure continuity and comparability.Evaluation reports should be designed to contain interesting and easily understandable materialfor many individuals and groups, including school staff, community members and families.Evaluation results can be used to initiate discussion, debate and proposals which can contributeto further development and support for healthy nutrition and for health promotion in schools.

5

Learning Physical Education

The outcomes in the Health and Physical Education learning area are interrelated and all contribute to the development of healthy, active lifestyles for students. Learning and teaching programs developed by teachers should allow students to learn and achieve the essential knowledge, attitudes and values and skills in an integrated manner: for example, a physical activity program may include knowledge of a game, the development of attitudes such as fair play and respect for the rights of others, and movement skills. It will also include interpersonal skills such as communication and conflict resolution for refereeing and team communication, and decision-making skills for choice of tactics and strategies. In a classroom context, a smoking education program might include essential knowledge about the effects of smoking, the development of values and the attitude that support the decision not to smoke and communication skills to cope with peer pressure to smoke.

Knowledge and Understanding

Through knowledge and understandings of key concepts, students are informed and take a critical perspective on health and physical activity issues within family, school, community and work settings.

Students know the essential health concepts and understand the importance of a balanced lifestyle that takes into account work, leisure and recreation. They know and understand, for example, vital concepts related to growth and development, physical activity and sport, food preparation and nutrition, mental health, sexuality, hygiene, communicable disease, relationships, drugs, personal safety and protective behaviours, sun protection, first aid and injury prevention. Students learn and understand the roles of relevant health agencies and how and when to access them. Students comprehend the various social, cultural, environmental and political factors that influence an individual's well-being and participation in physical activity. They understand, for example, how factors such as gender, culture and socioeconomic background might affect food choices or nutrition; how government initiatives might enhance sun protection; and how gender expectations or peers might influence participation in physical activity and sport. They recognise that not all groups in society have similar health status or access to health care, sport and recreational opportunities.

Students understand the importance of regular physical activity and its contribution to the quality of life of individuals and groups. They understand the principles of movement - how, when and why the body moves in certain ways - and use this knowledge to improve their movement skills. They know the rules, strategies, traditions and etiquettes of play, games, sport and recreation, and exhibit these understandings in physical activity. They appreciate the physical activity options that are available and that suit their needs in family, school, community and work contexts and critically analyse their physical activity preferences.

Attitudes and Values

Students identify attitudes and values for a healthy active, lifestyle and demonstrate values consistent with the prevention of ill-health, the acceptance of personal responsibility for their health and physical activity levels, respect for social justice principles and a commitment to personal achievement. For some students, religious insights will feature significantly in values acquisition and implementation.

Students acknowledge the value of regular physical activity and its contribution to health, by choosing to participate regularly in a variety of movement forms. They are willing participants in play, games, sport, adventure pursuits and recreational activities; for example, walking, cycling or doing tai chi or yoga in their daily routines.

Students value and demonstrate a commitment to the benefits of collaboration. They exhibit this in the classroom and in social and sporting settings: for example, they cooperate with others in planning rules for the classroom and contribute to the teamwork required for achievement of goals. They demonstrate a willingness to seek a compromise in situations in which conflicting views are evident, while protecting their own rights. They play fairly, abide by the rules and assist with equipment distribution and care.

Students recognise and value, safe and supportive environments. They demonstrate support for structures such as family, friendship groups, religious groups, support agencies and sporting teams. They support school policies such as a smoke-free environment, the prevention of bullying and a healthy canteen. They exhibit safe practice in the classroom, in play and in games, and observe occupational health and safety guidelines where appropriate.

Students recognise and respect the principles of social justice. They demonstrate this by being inclusive and just in their interpersonal relationships in classroom, peer, friendship and team situations. They know and protect their own rights and respect the rights of others. In physical activity and sport, they recognise inequities and do not discriminate on the grounds of gender, race, culture, physical or mental disability or experiential background. Their actions reflect ethical considerations and a desire to rectify inequities that exist in school, social and sporting settings. Students value the concept of personal excellence. They demonstrate this by striving for their personal best and acknowledging the achievements of others in class, social and physical activity settings.

Skills for Physical Activity

Students participate competently and confidently in physical activities such as play, games, sports, gymnastics, aquatics, dance, adventure pursuits and other active recreation.

They demonstrate fundamental movement skills of locomotion (e.g. walking, running and hopping), body management (e.g. balancing, tumbling and dodging) and object control (e.g. throwing, catching, striking and trapping) in free and structured play settings. They apply, extend and refine their fundamental movement skills and demonstrate this refinement in games, modified sports, sports and other recreational activities. They can combine fundamental movement patterns to create the more intricate movements required in play, games and recreation. They display coordinated movement, can move rhythmically to music and have optimum mobility and agility for their day-to-day living. They can also demonstrate skill in aquatic environments through swimming and water survival techniques.

Students apply these movement skills strategically in games, outdoor pursuits, dance and other recreational pursuits to enhance personal and group or team performance: for example, in games and sports, they demonstrate offensive and defensive tactics to reduce or prevent opposition scoring opportunities and enhance their own scoring potential. In outdoor pursuits, students plan strategically to determine factors such as the best route, mode of transport and necessary safety equipment when on an expedition. In gymnastics, they work strategically to improve their performance.

Self- Management Skills

Students demonstrate self-management skills such as decision making, goal setting, time management and stress management. They demonstrate these skills in all aspects of their lives, including family, school, careers, leisure and relationships. They set goals in the context of maintaining a healthy, active lifestyle. Students demonstrate the use of self-management skills to cope with the changing and often conflicting demands of a contemporary lifestyle. They are able to make decisions that guide practical actions for a healthy, active lifestyle, considering the influence of other people, media and advertising. They can demonstrate the use of these skills to plan and implement physical activity, manage stress and maintain their self-esteem.

Students apply a decision-making model to maintaining their personal health and the health of others. They make responsible decisions relating to issues such as personal hygiene, physical activity, drug use, nutrition and food preparation, relationships, healthy environments, injury prevention and personal safety and protective behaviours. They contribute to decision making for a healthy school environment and make informed choices about current and future education and employment options.

They plan and set short-and long-term goals to maintain and enhance their personal health and physical activity in areas of their lives such as family, school, careers, leisure and relationships. When participating in physical activity, they make strategic decisions that enhance personal and team performance. They can plan and monitor daily physical activity and fitness programs to meet the specific physical demands of a sport or daily living.

The students exert control over their lives through the application of time and stress management strategies: for example, they can keep a diary, prioritise changing and often conflicting demands and reflect on the effectiveness of their planning and modify their plans as required. When influenced by their peers, the media (especially advertising) or others to act in a manner contrary to their well-being, self-managed students assess the consequences of their behaviour, make informed decisions and choose courses of action that avoid risks and reduce harm.

Internpersonal Skills

Students possess the interpersonal skills of negotiation, assertiveness, conflict resolution, collaboration, cooperation and leadership in family, school, sport, work, cultural pursuits and social situations. They use these skills to interact effectively with others and to develop, maintain and end friendships and relationships.

Students demonstrate interpersonal skills in group-work and health promotion contexts: for example, assertive communication skills when making decisions about changing relationships, collaborative skills when planning and preparing a menu for a school camp, negotiation skills as part of a health committee promoting Heart Week throughout the school, and assertiveness skills when pressured by their peers. Students demonstrate interpersonal skills in groups and teams in roles such as participant, captain, leader, player, coach, manager or referee in sport, gymnastics and indoor or outdoor pursuits: for example, within a dance group students might exhibit leadership, communication, cooperation and negotiating skills when collaboratively choreographing a dance routine using the skills and strengths of the whole group.

A team captain uses leadership, communication and negotiation skills to ensure that the team tactics reflect fair play and utilise the individual skills of the players. In conflict situations, such as refereeing close games, the students use skills of conflict resolution and assertiveness to maintain effective control. Students in outdoor pursuits might cooperatively plan and implement an overnight bush walk that caters for all students in the group.

The Scope of the Curriculum

This section explains the scope of the curriculum which students might typically expect at four overlapping phases of development as a result of the implementation of the Health and Physical Education learning area outcomes. Examples are offered of the content and pedagogy that might be developed. The description is not meant to be prescriptive and it needs to be remembered that individual students progress at different rates. There will be many students whose curriculum experiences will be atypical because of their special needs or circumstances.

Teachers will need to make judgments about the particular content, emphasis and examples chosen at each phase of development. Their judgment will be influenced by factors such as:

— the values, attitudes and experiences of their students;

— the capabilities and ways of learning of their students; and

— the different cultural and geographical settings in which learning takes place.

Early Childhood

In the early childhood years, learning occurs in familiar contexts and settings which focus upon immediate events. In these situations, young children are provided with opportunities to optimise their health and safety knowledge, and to recognise that some people have different health needs. Through their involvement in play, games and physical activity (as well as through interactions with family, school and others), young children gain a clearer understanding of what it means to be healthy. They need to have learning experiences which are enjoyable and relevant. It is important at this phase of development that children learn about the stages and differences in human development, the factors which influence their choices of foods, activities and friends, and about the responsibilities of family members.

Young children learn how to keep themselves safe and to reduce risks to their health. The curricula should include knowledge, for example, about simple first aid procedures, warm-up and cool-down exercise procedures, sun protection and road safety. It should also include information about the rules and procedures of play and basic games. Children should be instructed in: the correct use of medicines; how to avoid harmful substances; personal hygiene; food preparation and nutrition; and the prevention of disease and illness.

Teachers can help children to understand the roles of people working in the health field, such as child care workers, school nurses and dental therapists.

Young children should be introduced to the value of physical activity and the benefits of regular and moderate exercise. Through play and games, they are physically active and realise that games and activities contribute to personal enjoyment and the formation of positive relationships with others.

Skills for physical activity are acquired developmentally, with fundamental movement skills providing the foundation for complex movement patterns and for more advanced activities. The emphasis during the early years of schooling should be on regular participation in cooperative, rather than competitive, physical activity.

Teachers act as facilitators and guides. They should recognise that individuals will be at different rates in their development and provide activities to allow children to enjoy success and participate with increasing confidence. Young children need a wide range of activities which are playful, fun, challenging and creative: for instance, students can be taught to move their bodies in different ways and respond to teacher directions to make different body shapes and explore ways of linking these movements.

In this early phase of development, students are able to practise fundamental movement skills, through parallel, individual and cooperative activities. They should be encouraged to develop efficient movement in locomotion (e.g. walking, running and hopping), body management (e.g. balancing, rolling and dodging) and object control activities (e.g. throwing, catching, kicking and striking).

A safe and supportive environment should be provided in which students can work, act, play and explore. Small and large play equipment is needed to enhance skills, coordination and enjoyment: for example, students can practise climbing under and over play equipment, throwing a beanbag into a hoop, rolling a ball between some markers, bouncing a ball on the ground, catching a large ball with two hands or hitting a small ball off a batting tee. To maximise participation and skill development, it is important that there be a high ratio of equipment to participants.

As skills and coordination develop, students learn to link movement patterns with greater success. Young children should be provided with opportunities to skip using a hand-held rope, or follow and repeat basic movements in dance in developing a simple routine. These safe, cooperative activities and simple games lead to the development of group and game strategies at later phases of development. Students learn to take turns, follow simple rules and share equipment and space. Spatial awareness can be developed through the use of simple games that involve dodging and chasing individually, in pairs, or in small groups.

Young children should be placed in situations in which they can observe, develop and explore self-management skills as individuals in class and friendship groups. They should practise decision-making, goalsetting and planning skills through play and interaction with peers, siblings and school community members.

Young children can learn the basic steps required to make decisions in familiar health and physical activity situations. With the assistance of adults, they are able make decisions and develop an understanding that more than one option often needs to be considered and that there are positive and negative consequences of their decision making. They develop awareness that they are constantly justifying their decisions and actions through situations such as play, food choices, personal hygiene, personal safety and friendships.

They should be provided with opportunities to explain to friends, a teacher or family member the basic strategies used to cope with unsafe situations or unhappy feelings. They should be given opportunities for maintaining their own personal safety in situations in which they may be harassed or bullied. It is in this phase of development that they should be introduced to the concept of time and time pressures through class routines, school programs and family responsibilities.

The provision of free and structured play, dance and structured skill development lessons will enable students, with the assistance of a adults, to begin to learn to monitor physical activity in their daily lives and relate this to their own play and activity levels.

Young children need opportunities and support to learn and value the interpersonal skills required to communicate and cooperate with peers and others in play, games, school and social situations.

Teaching and learning activities should focus on the fundamental communication skills of speaking clearly, listening to others without interruption, taking turns when speaking and listening and responding to clear instructions provided by the teacher. Children are encouraged to explore health issues; express their feelings openly and honestly; describe situations without undue exaggeration; recall key information (such as their name, address and phone number), and use the telephone effectively in emergency situations. They need to practise the use of verbal and non-verbal messages to communicate assertively, such as in play situations when a peer takes something from them, and in situations that make them feel uncomfortable.

Students are encouraged to cooperate with their peers in small group and play situations and achieve simple goals by sharing, caring, listening to others and taking turns. During play and games, they share space and equipment with others and ask politely if they may share these items with other children. They learn to follow the rules of an activity and to adjust these rules to ensure that everyone participates equally and fairly.

Children learn about their place in their family and social groups and how they can use their communication and cooperation skills to strengthen and maintain their relationships with family members, peers and the school community. At this phase of development, they begin to understand how these relationships change and how to use their interpersonal and self-management skills to cope with them.

Middle Childhood

In the middle childhood years, learning situations should provide opportunities for children to interact with peers in familiar and unfamiliar contexts and to further develop their understandings of concepts relating to a healthy life. Children build upon prior learning and experiences to gain a more detailed understanding of their personal health, growth and development, and the changes that occur from childhood, through puberty to adulthood. They examine the social and cultural factors which influence physical and mental health and further develop their understanding of the value of respect for the rights of others.

Opportunities need to be provided for investigating changing relationships with peers and individuals and children should been couraged to value the maintenance of positive relationships. Learning situations should provide practice in using strategies to manage physical, social and emotional changes (such as threatening behaviours and bullying), which lead to enhancement of their self-esteem and the esteem of others. These learning situations range from classroom to sporting contexts.

It is important to provide students with accurate information and to support the value of prevention of ill-health and the acceptance of personal responsibility for their health and physical activity. They should be provided with the opportunity to discuss processes of conception and birth, the responsibilities of parenting, the family and their changing role within the family.

They need to further develop their understanding of communicable diseases, including information about HIV/ AIDS and hepatitis. Students should learn about risk taking and explore strategies for avoiding or reducing harm associated with using common drugs and other harmful substances. They can practise skills for keeping themselves safe and protective behaviours that avoid or reduce risk, including identifying support networks such as Safety Houses and understanding the concepts of domestic violence and harassment. Their knowledge of injury prevention includes areas such as road use, safe bus and car travel, pedestrian and bicycle safety, water safety and sun protection.

Through class-based activities, students might, for example, examine the influence of the media and the images they present, and practise skills for managing that influence. Students should investigate how perceptions of mental illness, body shape or race influence the mental and emotional health of people or affect their individual rights.

Students should be given practice in appraising their physical activity levels and diet and learn to differentiate between forms of fitness. Concepts that underpin healthy food choices are elaborated and students can assess other factors that may impair their physical development and performance. Through their involvement in modified sports, gymnastics, dance, aquatics and outdoor pursuits, students learn about participation, basic game tactics, rules, safety procedures and how to avoid injury. These learning experiences enable them to feel comfortable in local community activities. They learn about and value the contribution that regular physical activity makes to their health.

Mastery of movement skills in the mid childhood years enables students to develop confidence and competence in specific skills for more complex physical activity. Teachers should provide opportunities for regular physical activity in the form of games, modified sports, dance, gymnastics, fitness, water safety and outdoor pursuits. Students optimise their safe performance through learning and using safe practices and basic strategies and tactics that lead to success in physical activity environments.

Children recognise individual differences in rates of development and readiness. They should practise, extend and refine skills in a variety of activities that progressively challenge them physically: for example, they might begin to consider the principles of movement when throwing or kicking a ball, to control speed, distance and direction. Likewise, individuals need time to practise the skill of maintaining possession of the ball with stick, hand or foot while changing speed and direction, or creating a dance sequence. Balance in lesson planning needs to be maintained between individual, pair, cooperative and competitive activities, and group and team practices. Lesson planning should reflect the prior learning experiences of the students.

Children can apply their knowledge of rules by thinking strategically to implement individual strategies to achieve goals and enhance performance in activities such as Netta Netball, Rooball, orienteering and creative dance. It is recommended that these game strategies be practised in a variety of contexts.

Children continue to develop their self-management skills and personal strengths. They gain feedback from others to enhance their health, physical activity and selfesteem. Through practice, they extend their decision-making skills to predict and meet personal needs, while seeking help from others when necessary. Children learn to consider a broader range of alternatives and see the longer-term consequences of their decision-making, goalsetting and stress management. In real and role-play situations, they develop an increasing ability to recognise positive and negative consequences of their decisions: for example, choosing not to smoke because they realise its effect on sporting performance.

They should be provided with the opportunity to justify their choices, contribute to group decision making and set realistic and measurable short-term goals. Such activities assist students to differentiate between types of goals and to practise prioritising their tasks, goals and responsibilities. Through these learning experiences students become more skilled at being able to predict situations in which they are likely to feel stressed or threatened and to develop strategies for coping with these pressures.They learn to actively manage their time, including scheduling time for homework, rest, after-school sport, recreation and family activities.

Through being given the opportunity to participate in a wide variety of physical activities, students begin to identify the types of physical activity and sport they prefer. They experience high, moderate and low levels of physical activity and monitor their own physical activity levels and those of others and practise relating these to different aspects of personal fitness. Time needs to be allocated for students to plan regular physical activity in their daily lives, such as walking to school, surfing or playing modified sports. By making strategic decisions, such as applying basic offensive and defensive tactics in a modified sport, students are able to optimise their individual and team performance. At this phase of their development, students are able to extend their understanding of the factors that affect their identity and learn that decisions they make have positive and negative influences on their self-esteem. They can examine the impact that changes, have on their self-esteem. They can begin to understand how the influence of stereotyping and comments from significant others affect their self-esteem and identity. Students learn and practise self-management skills to cope with these influences.

The continued development of students' interpersonal skills is vital. Children should be encouraged to communicate their feelings about change, resolve conflict and contribute actively to the achievement of group goals. Such activities will assist them to communicate effectively with infants, their peers, adults and the aged.

Children should learn to expand their negotiation and facilitation skills to help others and to enhance and maintain relationships in group and social situations. Through situations such as group discussions and role-play scenarios on relevant health issues children can learn and practise communication and cooperation skills. There should be opportunities to speak assertively, discuss their feelings, use appropriate language to discuss sensitive health issues, disagree with others without getting angry, and resolve conflict.

Children are able to use their interpersonal skills to develop and maintain support networks with trusted adults. Children can develop empathy through learning to praise and support others when they make mistakes. The refinement of such skills assists them to respond positively to advice and constructive criticism while maintaining their self-esteem. By learning and practising group discussion skills and procedures, children are able to use their communication and decision making skills to assist a group to collaboratively plan and achieve goals in games, modified sports and recreation.

There are various opportunities within the school environment for students to demonstrate their interpersonal skills to enhance the operation or outcome of a game or activity and a group or team's performance. They need to be given time to practise leadership and display initiative in organised games and activities, scoring and refereeing, and setting out equipment.They should be encouraged to consider and value the abilities and feelings of others in games and actualise this through actions such as pitching more slowly to a batter of lesser ability, or learning to give and receive advice to improve their own and others' performance.

When conflict occurs, students should learn to use their assertive communication and conflict-resolution skills to maintain the activity or game. They should learn to appreciate the role of officials and to better use their interpersonal skills to encourage others to accept the rules and codes of behaviour of a class or a game. They should be able to communicate their feelings appropriately in challenging situations, such as winning or losing a close game.

Early Adolescence

In the early adolescent years, students are concerned with the contemporary issues facing them and the local community. Therefore learning in this phase of development should be focused on understanding the complex factors affecting their own well-being and that of others in both familiar and unfamiliar contexts. Students should be provided with strategies for maintaining their health and physical activity levels and they should be able to realistically appraise the health and fitness levels of themselves and others. They need to understand that health status is influenced by social, cultural and environmental factors, such as public health policy and socioeconomic status.

Students build on prior knowledge about growth and development. They should be provided with opportunities to discuss the physical, mental, emotional and social changes associated with growth and development. They need to acquire knowledge about the processes of conception, pregnancy, childbirth and ageing. They should learn about the benefits of intimate and group relationships and how to cope with factors that may influence the maintenance of self-esteem of others and themselves in these relationships. To maintain and enhance their own wellbeing, it is important that adolescents be well informed about the impact of stress on health and about strategies to manage stress. Students should be provided with information and strategies on how to cope with changes in mental and emotional states such as grief, loss and the breakdown of relationships. They should be provided with opportunities to discuss important issues such as suicide prevention and abuse and mental health and mental illness.

In early adolescence, students need to develop strategies for reducing risks associated with certain lifestyle behaviours. Teachers should provide advice about how to avoid lifestyle diseases, including heart disease and communicable diseases (e.g. HIV/AIDS, sexually-transmitted diseases and hepatitis). Young adolescents should be made aware of the benefits of moderate physical activity, sound diet, engaging in safe behaviours and the dangers associated with taking risks such as driving under the influence of alcohol. They need to be able to view the media critically and to carefully analyse the messages and information which are conveyed in relation to nutrition, drugs, sexual activity and relationships. It is important that students become competent in basic first aid and realise both the variety of contexts in which these skills might be required e.g. home, workplace, sporting field and highway and the range of injuries related to alcohol and other drugs.

Students should continue to learn about and develop individual and team strategies to enhance performance. They should become increasingly familiar with the roles and responsibilities required within team structures. They can learn to design physical activity programs which access community recreation and sporting facilities and understand that participation in such activities can be influenced by factors such as cost and geographic location. They should learn the rules and etiquettes associated with selected sports. When placed in a variety of contexts, they can develop strategies for the safety of others in physical activities or in the workplace.

Teachers should continue to provide opportunities for safe, regular physical activity for all students. In early adolescence, students are encouraged to pursue their specific physical activity interests and participate in fewer physical activity contexts. They develop higher levels of skill by applying the principles of movement. School programs should provide choice from a variety of individual and team sports, dance, outdoor pursuits and recreation, and ensure that all students have the opportunity to learn to be safe in anaquatic environment. Through participation, students are able to develop high-level physical activity skills which, in turn, make them confident participants in community sport, recreation or performance festivals.

Students should have opportunities to react to challenges provided by the environment (e.g. playing into the wind in tennis) or opposing players (e.g. block in volleyball). In individual and group situations, they learn to develop and implement strategies within established etiquette and rules to optimise performance in games, sports and other activities: for example, students learn to modify a dance to complement the music, switch the play in hockey or modify the route in hiking to suit the terrain and ability of the students.

Students are encouraged to examine and apply their self-management skills to the planning of short-term and longer-term health and physical activity goals. With practice they can effectively utilise these skills to cope with changing and challenging situations and to provide support for others. Students should apply the decision-making process in a variety of familiar and unfamiliar situations. They should be able to analyse the processes and outcomes of decision-making, taking into account their values and those of others (e.g. the media). Students are assisted in developing decision making skills through role-play situations such as justifying and informing others of their choices (e.g. choosing non-alcoholic drinks at peers' parties), discussing drug issues with parents or refereeing a sport. Through class activities such as these, students can empathise with and consider the views of others in their own decision making.

Students continue to monitor their own physical activity levels, as well asest ablishing and improving their fitness profiles. Through opportunities to participate in sport, outdoor pursuits, recreation and dance, they learn how to set and evaluate goals for participation and personal excellence and make strategic decisions to optimise team or group performance: for example, they can change their defensive strategy in response to opposition tactics.

Through the outdoor expedition experience, students are able to plan effectively for their personal and group mode of travel, sustenance and safety, while ensuring achievement of group goals and maintenance of the natural environment. Students should be provided with opportunities to develop the ability and confidence to deal with influences (such as discrimination, media, work, love, grief, stress and membership of certain groups, such as clubs and sporting teams) which impact upon their self-confidence, self esteem and self-identify. With practice, young adolescents can develop personal monitoring skills to regulate their behaviour. They can translate these influences into positive actions such as accessing people or agencies to over come stereotypes and discrimination that affect their personal and professional aspirations.

Students should be encouraged to use their interpersonal skills to assertively communicate their personal health and physical activity decisions, particularly when exposed to unwanted peer influence or other pressure. They should continue to develop their negotiation skills. Students need to acquire the interpersonal skills necessary to develop, maintain and cope with changes in relationships, such as those in family, marriage, parenting and intimate and other social situations. Students should practise developing their own group management skills by being members of a group, team or committee. They should use their interpersonal skills to assertively communicate decisions to others on relevant health issues such as sport and food choices or refusing unwanted sexual activity.

Students become increasingly comfortable with joining new groups and initiating and maintaining conversation. They should be assisted in further developing their assertiveness, negotiation and conflict resolution skills to enable them to cope with change and conflict situations in which emotions may be involved. These skills are effective in developing, maintaining or possibly challenging relationships in which power, gender, race, or culture are used to empower or disempower others. Through school situations they may increasingly demonstrate group management skills, using their interpersonal skills to resolve conflict and facilitate effective communication and cooperation in groups.

In team, sporting or group physical activity situations, students can learn to interact and work effectively with less-familiar people and to manage challenging or difficult situations, such as 'ugly' spectators in sport. They have opportunities to display initiative and leadership by organising and managing group or team activities such as selecting teams, scoring, refereeing, deciding on a safe hiking route or leading a new dance routine. Students should learn to compromise and use negotiation skills to manage disputes, facilitate active involvement of all participants and solve problems. As group leaders, referees or captains, they can display fairness and adherence to rules and codes of conduct and observe minimal-impact practice in sensitive environmental conditions.

Late Adolscence/Young Adulthood

Young adults have the ability to act independently and take increasing responsibility for their own learning. Learning situations focus on reviewing and reflecting on decisions made and actions taken. They also critically analyse their own and others' beliefs about health issues. Young adults are concerned with their post school destinations and have opportunities to specialise in their studies. They choose courses which reflect their interests and abilities, and their anticipated educational and vocational directions. Post-compulsory subjects and programs in this learning area focus on health and physical activity, personal development, beliefs and values systems, early childhood parenting skills, skills to assist movement into independent living situations and career pathways.

Students learn to live and assist others in harmony with the natural environment. Knowledge and Understandings Adolescents should be provided with opportunities to explore the complex social, cultural, environmental and political influences on the health status of individuals and groups within society. Learning situations should focus on contexts that require students to demonstrate analytical skills and strategies in response to perceived and actual influences affecting the health and safety needs of populations. Students now have their own strategies for making judgments and decisions.

Through their selection of courses they are introduced to more complex research methods (especially those using technology) and are able to collect information about health initiatives and physical activity from a range of sources. They can critically examine the effects of programs on individuals and groups within the community, such as the aged or special groups whose experiences disadvantage them. Through learning and teaching programs they are able to consider laws and policies and develop strategies to effect change where necessary. In the school context they are able to plan site-based health promotion campaigns. Students develop strategies to avoid harm and manage changes that may cause stress in their lives, such as unwanted pregnancies or suicidal feelings, and they actively evaluate the effects of these strategies.

Adolescents face particular pressures related to school performance and parental and peer expectations. They should further develop their understanding of stress management techniques and be encouraged to adopt a lifestyle which balances their work commitments with maintaining a healthy and active lifestyle that includes active or passive recreational pursuits.

They can examine the development of infants, identify their needs and interact with young children to practise skills that should assist with parenting. Adolescents learn to accurately assess the physical activity needs of themselves and others and independently plan strategies to enhance their involvement in community activity and recreation programs. They are taught to design physical-activity programs to enhance the fitness and health of groups within the community (such as seniors, disabled students and adults with poor activity patterns) and to analyse the influence of these plans.

They can learn to apply biomechanical principles to the development of the movement skills of themselves and others. They learn how community values or affluence influence the provision of services for health and recreation needs and compare the levels of service between different communities.

Adolescents are able to refine physical activity skills and work towards achieving their personal best by participating in sporting teams, outdoor pursuits, dance festivals and other community physical activities. Schools continue to promote participation in regular, moderate, physical activity for all students by providing choice from a variety of individual or team sports, dance and outdoor pursuits. By the time they have reached this phase of development, most adolescents have the skills to succeed in community physical activity settings. Through the use of movement analysis techniques (including the application of technology), students are able to analyse and develop high-level movement skills that are specific to the pressures of competitive sport or other performance situations. They learn to compare the movement skills of themselves and their peers with those performing at a high level in the community. They can participate safely in wilderness expeditions and their sporting skills are sufficient for them to successfully perform in community senior sport.

In challenging physical activity settings, adolescents learn strategic skills that can be further refined. They effectively evaluate the outcomes of their strategies to optimise individual and group performance. They learn to devise, implement and evaluate detailed game plans in sport to respond to the strengths and weaknesses of opponents. In outdoor pursuits, students attain the competence to navigate with precision in difficult terrain and evaluate the challenges provided by the prevailing environment. In dance, students learn to strategically plan, for example, school participation in a rock eisteddfod. Students also learn to analyse and develop risk management strategies in different situations, promoting safety for themselves and others.

Adolescents learn sophisticated self-management skills in complex situations and practise analysis of them. They plan actions to manage social and cultural influences on self-esteem. They learn to critically evaluate decisions made in complex situations; for example, assessing the effect of policies and changes in social and cultural identity on the self-esteem of population groups, including those with specific needs. Their considerations include the values, feelings and needs of themselves and others.

They refine their negotiation, decision making, planning and goal-setting skills and evaluate these processes in emotional and complex situations (such as within intimate relationships), where the values and needs of others must be considered. They critically evaluate the impact of social and political decisions on the well-being of individuals and population groups. They analyse time-management and stress management strategies in terms of their lifestyle to support physical, mental and emotional health. They develop detailed action plans to achieve post-school work related goals and evaluate the consequences of such plans. They plan health promotion programs in areas such as drug education and road trauma, and consider the values of different groups.

Adolescents can interpret fitness data and plan, implement and evaluate a training program to improve a component of fitness (e.g. strength) for themselves, an Èlite sport or a special population group. By applying the principles of movement and using technology, they can set goals and implement and evaluate strategies to improve their physical skill performance in a sport or recreational activity. Young adults learn about the influence of social and cultural factors on the self-esteem of themselves and population groups: for example, through the critical analysis of the impact of gender and cultural stereotyping on career options, they learn how to manage their own self-esteem and support the development of the self-esteem of others. They learn to evaluate personal and health agency strategies to develop and maintain self-esteem. They assess the impact of factors such as long-term unemployment, serious injury or disability and mental and emotional health and illness on personal identity and understand the relationship between long-term loss of identity and health.

Adolescents continue to develop sound interpersonal skills which enable them to contribute to group activities, resolve conflict and cope with changes in intimate and other relationships. Through analysis of their own and others' interpersonal skills, they can improve their relationship skills and participate, lead and manage group activities more effectively. In role-play and group discussions, students analyse and refine the interpersonal skills necessary to start, maintain and end relationships, considering their own feelings while showing empathy and respect for the feelings of others. Students use these skills to provide support for peers in discussing and resolving health issues of concern. Adolescents build upon their skills of critical analysis of relationships, communication and leadership to optimise health and physical activity choices. They may do this individually or as part of group planning. They learn to take social action to reduce disadvantage or inequity for others in the school community. Individual students, for instance, may encourage others to be physically active and maintain a healthy diet. A group of students might undertake advocacy for the introduction of a school drug policy, or be involved in a school hiking expedition or a physical activity promotion.

Students use their interpersonal skills to communicate effectively with employers and colleagues in the workplace. They use their communication skills to raise awareness of and resolve occupational health and safety issues in their work environment. As leaders in the school community, students learn to plan and monitor the progress of their group, facilitate group decision making and evaluate group performance against the group goals: for example, they might learn to organise school activities to promote awareness of sun protection in National Skin Cancer Week.

Adolescents extend their interpersonal skills to develop relationships that enable them to make a long-term commitment to a team or group activity as a participant, player, captain, leader, coach or referee. They have increased opportunities to contribute to team harmony and spirit through their leadership or actions. When coaching a junior team, they exhibit leadership and acceptable sporting behaviour in winning and losing situations.They are able to take social action, either individually or as members of groups, for advocacy of increased physical activity opportunities in the community. They may, for example, approach the school staff and local government authority to improve after-school recreation opportunities for themselves or others.

Learning, Teaching & Assessment

The Overarching Statement provides general advice about learning, teaching and assessment based on understandings about how students learn best in outcomes-focused education. This section builds on this advice in the context of the Health and Physical Education learning area. Additional information is provided on evaluating attitudes and values.

Learning and Teaching

Learning experiences should enable students to observe and practise the actual processes, products, skills and values which are expected of them. Students should be provided with the opportunity to acquire the essential knowledge and understandings about a healthy lifestyle, to acquire and practise physical activity skills and to develop the attitudes and values which are promoted in this learning area. Students learn most effectively when they have opportunities to observe health practices and values being modelled and promoted. They should be provided with a range of purposeful activities that stimulate thought and inquiry and are enjoyable. Students should be able to apply and practise the processes, skills and values which are expected of them in a variety of contexts, both within and outside the classroom: for example, they can make responsible decisions about the type of physical activity in which they might participate and plan and develop game skills or a healthy diet.

Connection and challenge

— *Opportunity to learn:* Learning experiences should connect with students' existing knowledge, skills and values while extending and challenging their current ways of thinking and acting.

Effective learning in the Health and Physical Education Learning Area involves making connections between students' knowledge, skills, attitudes, values and experiences. Students are able to learn effectively when they are able to link and apply elements of the curriculum within and across different learning areas in meaningful ways, for example, students can identify what constitutes independent living or decision-making skills in health contexts or physical activity and apply these in a range of situations. Learning activities will provide students with opportunities to progressively develop and extend their knowledge, understanding and skills to become healthy individuals with the ability and condidence to manage their own lifestyles. Learning and teaching opportunities should be provided for students to challenge their ways of thinking and acting; for example, they should be asked to question stereotypes, challenge media images and debate the views of their peers and others on a variety of health issues. Challenges should be within the reach of students and will vary for student to student, particularly in relation to physical activity and sport. Care needs to be taken to ensure that the gap between students' existing knowledge and the new challenge is not too great.

— *Action and reflection:* Learning experiences should be meaningful and encourage both action and reflection on the part of the learner.

Students should participate in and practise activities that encourage and assist the development of a healthy active lifestyle. These activities should enable students to apply their knowledge and skills in a holistic and realistic way in individual and group situations.

Teachers in the role of facilitators or coaches should use a student-centred approach. Students are encouraged to act, reflect and monitor their own performance, enabling them to identify their strengths and develop practices to improve their performances; for example, prior to the conclusion of an activity such as a small-group discussion on a health issue or a physical activity, teachers can facilitate debriefings to encourage students to reflect on their own and others' performance. The action and reflection process supports the development of values such as acceptance of personal responsibility, commitment to the benefits of collaboration and striving for personal improvement.

— *Motivation and purpose:* Learning experiences should be motivating and their purpose clear to the student.

Students should be motivated to achieve their personal best. Activities should focus on the outcomes and enhance meaning and enjoyment in learning. Teaching and learning situations should provide opportunities for individual cooperation and competitive challenges where appropriate. Activities should be structured so that individuals of varying abilities can develop their knowledge, skills and values. Students need to be clear about what they are learning and why and how they can take responsibility for their own learning. This can best be achieved when they are involved in the planning of health, physical activity and sport programs and in the design and implementation of assessment strategies. Teachers act as facilitators by working with students on health issues which are of concern to them and balance this with information from the family and the broader community gained through methods such as parent surveys, research, reports and local statistics on health issues. Self directed learning is complemented by other approaches, including explicit teaching about contemporary health or physical activity issues.

— *Inclusivity and difference:* Learning experiences should respect and accommodate differences between learners.

When planning and implementing learning and teaching activities for students, it is important to acknowledge that each individual is different. These differences may be due to a variety of influences, including health, culture, family background, beliefs, values, gender and ability. These differences, while requiring students and teachers to be accepting and sensitive, can stimulate rich and varied discussion on a wide range of health issues.

Students also differ in their rates of learning and learning styles. Therefore the teaching and learning program should take into account the students' physical, mental, spiritual and emotional development. Priority health issues and physical activities should be structured so that all students feel comfortable and confident in participating. Each student needs to be challenged but the nature of the challenge may vary from student to student, particularly in relation to physical activity and sport; for example, the development of movement skills can be facilitated by a range of play, physical education and sporting activities that provide opportunities for students with high and low abilities to improve. Students with disabilities should be provided with appropriate, alternative avenues for achieving the outcomes. In physical activities students with low ability may not achieve when only involved in group activities with high-ability students.

Prior learning of students needs to be valued and students should be encouraged to strive for personal excellence.

— *Autonomy and collaboration:* Learning experiences should encourage students to learn both independently and from and with others.

Learning experiences should be regularly provided which encourage students to learn both individually and collaboratively. Students should be encouraged to take responsibility for their own learning and to become independent learners by choosing ways of exploring health issues and improving their skills and participation in a range of physical activities. They can work individually to ensure personal understandings of concepts and processes and the development of movement skills. Working in groups enables students to be challenged by the views and skills of others and extends their abilities to handle collaboration and competition, conflict and teamwork.

Learning is most effective when students can make links between the classroom, school, community, work and home environments through their involvement in clubs, recreation, sport, dance, community service or outdoor pursuits. To optimise student learning it is important that parents and carers are aware of the content of programs and the values endorsed by the school community.

— *Supportive environment:* The school and classroom setting should be safe and conducive to effective learning.

A supportive environment enables students to optimise their performance in health, physical activity and sport. Programs should promote maximum participation by students and a sense of achievement. Teachers should ensure that students are provided with a safe environment and adequately supervised at all times, particularly when participating in physical activities. Competitive situations should be well organised and managed by appropriate umpires and referees.

Classroom learning activities are reinforced by including supportive school procedures, structures and policies: for example, wearing hats for sun protection; promoting sound nutrition through the canteen; and demonstrating respect and concern for others and their rights through school pastoral care programs. Schools may provide opportunities for students to be consulted or actively involved during the development of these policies. Behaviours which contribute to a safe environment free from injury or harassment are modelled by staff and students and supported by parents. Students who are given work placements as part of their learning experience should complete an injury-specific occupational safety, health and welfare certificate.

Assessment

Valid

Assessment should provide valid information on the actual ideas, processes, products and values which are expected of students. Assessment items should accurately test what they are supposed to test and provide students with the opportunity to demonstrate the achievement of one or more of the learning outcomes. For example, observation of student performance in a game of badminton will provide information on the achievement of the outcomes for physical activity and interpersonal skills.

Assessment should allow a summative judgement over time about the student's achievement on an outcome. For example, judgement about student attainment of the knowledge and understandings outcome should be based on student performance in a number of different health contexts in order to provide sufficient data to confirm the achievement of the outcomes.

Educative

Assessment should make a positive contribution to students learning. Assessment practices should assist students to reflect on and evaluate their performance and what they have learned in a variety of health and physical education contexts. In physical activity contexts students may analyse their achievements towards the appropriate outcomes, identify their strengths and weaknesses, plan a program of improvement and monitor the implementation and outcomes of the plan. They would use this information to analyse their performance and adjust learning and improvement goals as necessary.

In health contexts students may review the curriculum outcomes in relation to their understandings and skills, research further information on the health issue to improve their understanding and to identify issues that require clarification with peers or the class teacher.

Explicit

Assessment criteria should be explicit so that the basis for judgements is clear and public. Students should be made aware if judgements are being made about their attainment of physical skills, their level of participation or their understanding of a key concept or a comination of these. The criteria for all forms of assessment needs to be established as a matter of fairness to the students. For example students engaged in decision making activities are clearly aware of the criteria which will be used to monitor their skills.

Fair

Assessment should be demonstrably fair to all students and not discriminate on grounds that are irrelevant to the achievement of the outcomes. Assessment should be sensitive and responsive to differences that exist among students so that students are not favoured or disadvantaged in demonstrating their achievement of an outcome. What are familiar or helpful contexts for some students will be unfamiliar or unhelpful to others. Fair assessment often means assessing the one outcome in different ways related to the characteristics and circumstances of particular students. For example, developing alternative assessment strategies for students with physical disabilities; or recognising the socio-economic and cultural influences on students' food choices.

Comprehensive

Judgements on student progress should be based on multiple kinds and sources of evidence. This will necessitate gathering a variety of information based on a range of tasks to make judgements about a particular outcome(s). For example, anecdotal records (such as level of participation), work folios and personal diaries could be used to monitor skills for physical activity. Assessment should be conducted in contexts that resemble real life situations (when monitoring health practices and attitudes) through the use of role-play, charades, puppets, debates and panel discussions.

Students understand how culture influences the food people eat and how people value themselves and participate in physical activity. Students make decisions about a healthy and active lifestyle based on examination of social, cultural, environmental and political issues associated with health. They develop their understanding of other cultures through the music and dances of other countries.

Through interaction with people from other cultural groups, students learn about the values and views of other groups and appreciate the sporting achievements of other countries. When reviewing dietary habits, they appreciate the contribution that other cultures have made in regard to dietry habits.

Students understand the importance of taking into account the artistic, cultural and intellectual work of others when they participate in physical activity and creative solutions in play, games and sports; create and present dance routines; and respond to rhythm through movement.

Students examine the physical, mental, emotional and social development of the individual and the impact of interactions between the individual, the wider community and the environment on the health of populations. They acquire understandings, attitudes and values which are essential for promoting health practices and which encourage participation in regular physical activity and the adoption of a well-balanced lifestyle, taking into account work, leisure and rest. They set and achieve personal goals; plan, implement and evaluate decisions; maintain and enhance self-esteem; improve relationships; manage stress; and cope with change. They use skills to safeguard and enhance their physical and mental health and to plan for their future. Students acquire movement skills and gain a sense of achievement when performing physical activity. This in turn promotes participation in sport and recreation as lifelong pursuits.

Students become aware of the important roles that motivation, enthusiasm, selfdiscipline, self-respect, cooperation and the assumption of responsibility play in the learning process. This approach leads to self-confidence and self-direction in setting and achieving goals. Effective interpersonal skills are learned and practised to enable students to act responsibly and contribute effectively to groups and teams. Students who learn physical activity skills in a safely-controlled environment perform confidently in play, games, sport and dance and become highly motivated to strive for excellence, either individually or in a collaborative team setting

Students recognise and comment on safe practices and are able to recognise safe people and safe houses. They know their rights and understand and value the obligations associated with particular health issues such as sexuality, hygiene, communicable diseases, relationships, drugs, personal safety, sun protection, injury prevention, first aid, road safety, tobacco smoke and car exhaust fumes. Students know the rights and responsibilities of employers and employees in regard to occupational safety, health and welfare. They are encouraged to show respect for social justice principles and the rights and ability levels of others in group discussion, games, play or sport. Students value the talents of the elite performer in competitive situations. Students make decisions that allow them to manage stress, report domestic violence or harassment by peers.

Links with Other Learning Areas

The Health and Physical Education learning area draws on some of the understandings, elements, processes and skills of arts forms developed in The Arts: for example, rhythmic gymnastics, callisthenics and aerobics use elements of music to create different movement responses. Students use elements of visual arts to promote health-enhancing behaviours or when presenting ideas related to food preparation and nutrition, growth and development or safety.

The Health and Physical Education learning area contributes to the achievement by students of most of the English learning area outcomes. The use of appropriate language in different contexts is encouraged: for example, language used in a family context would normally be different from that used when umpiring or being interviewed by an employer to obtain work experience. Language has an important effect on self-esteem and confidence, and the use of appropriate language is critical to the development of a healthy mental state. The ways in which parents, teachers, peers, media or literature communicate information, attitudes, values and particular beliefs can have a marked impact on individuals when they are making responsible decisions about a healthy lifestyle.

Students have the opportunity to appreciate the way in which language and culture associated with games, sport, food or leisure activities contribute to the Australian way of life. Students identify the difficulties people have in understanding promotional messages relating to health and safety in a second language context and explore alternative forms of communication when appropriate. Students apply numeracy skills when they score in various games, activities and pursuits. They learn about the dimensions of playing fields and court sizes, the period of time played, the number of members of a team and the space in which they should move for successful play.

They calculate averages, medians and the differences between high and low performances to compare their own performance to that of others. They use graphs to make observations, interpretations and inferences in relation to weather patterns and navigation conventions for orienteering and outdoor pursuits. They use statistical procedures when researching health-related concepts. Students use common measuring equipment, such as clocks, tapes and scales, and they cost and measure food quantities and calculate food preparation, cooking and serving times.

One of the strongest links is with the Science learning area. The knowledge and understandings of the physical, biological and natural worlds are complementary to both learning areas. Students investigate the physical, mental, emotional and environmental variables that affect their state of well-being. They examine the preparation of foods and the changes made to them by heating, freezing, boiling, microwaving and sterilising to kill bacteria, avoid diseases and prevent infection. Students discuss scientific processes and products of science and their effect on people and their environment. They form reasoned judgments about issues such as recycling, advertising of food products, garment labelling, in-vitro fertilisation programs, the use and misuse of the environment or the taking of steroids to enhance performance. They apply science in their daily lives in regard to health and hygiene, in the home, school or community.

The Health and Physical Education learning area outcomes relate to a number of Society and Environment outcomes. Students plan and carry out investigations about the way people interact with each other and their environments in order to draw conclusions about desirable self-management and interpersonal skills.

Students examine the consequences of cultural and environmental changes on the physical, mental, emotional and social well-being of the individual. They make informed decisions about food, clothing, shelter, safety and social relationships that suit their needs in family, school, community and work contexts.

Students examine the effects of social, political, environmental and cultural factors on community health and consider public health issues and initiatives on immunisation and the control of communicable diseases. Active citizenship is promoted in such matters as respect for the laws and regulations relating to road safety, drug and alcohol use and smoking, as well as the assumption of unpaid responsibilities in sporting and recreational clubs.

The skills and understandings developed in the Technology and Enterprise learning area are utilised and enhanced in the Health and Physical Education learning area. Students access, select and use materials which promote health enhancing environments in the home, school, community or workplace. They also consider modification of these materials to suit people at different stages of their life cycle or people with physical disabilities. Students understand concepts relating to complexities of systems operating in organised ways: for example, the reaction of body systems to physical activity, dietary habits and drug use; or behaviour patterns out of harmony with a personal belief system that can lead to a destructive mental state. Students apply operational, manipulative and organisational skills when selecting and using technology.

International Charter of Physical Education and Sport

(Adopted by the General Conference at its twentieth session, Paris, 21 November 1978)

Preamble

The General Conference of the United Nations Educational, Scientific and Cultural Organization, meeting in Paris at its twentieth session, this twenty-first day of November 1978.

Recalling that in the United Nations Charter the peoples proclaimed their faith in fundamental human rights and in the dignity and worth of the human person and affirmed their determination to promote social progress and better standards of life,

Recalling that by the terms of the Universal Declaration of Human Rights everyone is entitled to all the rights and freedoms set forth therein without discrimination of any kind as to race, colour, sex, language, religion, political or other opinion, national or social origin, property, birth or other consideration,

Convinced that one of the essential conditions for the effective exercise of human rights is that everyone should be free to develop and preserve his or her physical, intellectual and moral powers, and that access to physical education and sport should consequently be assured and guaranteed for all human beings,

Convinced that to preserve and develop the physical. intellectual and moral powers of the human being improves the quality of life at the national and the international levels,

Believing that physical education and sport should make a more effective contribution to the inculcation of fundamental human values underlying the full development of peoples, Stressing accordingly that physical education and sport should seek to promote closer communion between peoples and between individuals. together with disinterested emulation, solidarity and fraternity, mutual respect and understanding, and full respect for the integrity and dignity of human beings,

Considering that responsibilities and obligations are incumbent upon the industrialized countries and the developing countries alike for reducing the disparity which continues to exist between them in respect of free and universal access to physical education and sport,

Considering that to integrate physical education and sport in the natural environment is to enrich them and to inspire respect of the earth's resources and a concern to conserve them and use them for the greater good of humanity as a whole,

Taking into account the diversity of the forms of training and education existing in the world, but noting that, notwithstanding the differences between national sports structures, it is clearly evident that physical education and sport are not confined to physical well-being and health but also contribute to the full and well-balanced development of the human being,

Taking into account, furthermore, the enormous efforts that have to be made before the right to physical education and sport can become a reality for all human beings, Stressing the importance for peace and friendship among peoples of co-operation between the international governmental and non-governmental organizations responsible for physical education and sport,

Proclaims this International Charter for the purpose of placing the development of physical education and sport at the service of human progress, promoting their development, and urging governments, competent non-governmental organizations, educators, families and individuals themselves to be guided thereby, to disseminate it and to put it into practice.

Article 1. The practice of physical education and sport is a fundamental right for all

1.1. Every human being has a fundamental right of access to physical education and sport, which are essential for the full development of his personality. The freedom to develop physical, intellectual and moral powers through physical education and sport must be guaranteed both within the educational system and in other aspects of social life.

1.2. Everyone must have full opportunities, in accordance with his national tradition of sport, for practising physical education and sport. developing his physical fitness and attaining a level of achievement in sport which corresponds to his gifts.

1.3. Special opportunities must be made available for young people, including children of pre-school age, for the aged and for the handicapped to develop their personalities to the full through physical education and sport programmes suited to their requirements.

Article 2. Physical education and sport for an essential element of lifelong education in the overall education system

2.1. Physical education and sport, as an essential dimension of education and culture, must develop the abilities, will-power and self-discipline of every human being as a fully integrated member of society. The continuity of physical activity and the practice of sports must be ensured throughout life by means of a global, lifelong and democratized education.

2.2. At the individual level, physical education and sport contribute to the maintenance and improvement of health, provide a wholesome leisure-time occupation and enable man to overcome the drawbacks of modern living. At the community level, they enrich social relations and develop fair play. which is essential not only to sport itself but also to life in society.

2.3. Every overall education system must assign the requisite place and importance to physical education and sport in order to establish a balance and strengthen links between physical activities and other components of education.

Article 3. Physical education and sport programmes must meet individual and social needs

3.1. Physical education and sport programmes must be designed to suit the requirements and personal characteristics of those practising them, as well as the institutional, cultural, socio-economic and climatic conditions of each country. They must give priority to the requirements of disadvantaged groups in society.

3.2. In the process of education in general, physical education and sport programmes must, by virtue of both their content and their timetables, help to create habits and behaviour patterns conducive to full development of the human person.

3.3. Even when it has spectacular features, competitive sport must always be in accordance with the Olympic ideal to serve the purpose of educational sport, of which it represents the crowning epitome. It must in no way be influenced by profit-seeking commercial interests.

Article 4. Teaching, coaching and administration of physical education and sport should be performed by qualified personnel

4.1. All personnel who assume professional responsibility for physical education and sport must have appropriate qualifications and training. They must be carefully selected in sufficient numbers and given preliminary as well as further training to ensure that they reach adequate levels of specialization.

4.2. Voluntary personnel, given appropriate training and supervision, can make an invaluable contribution to the comprehensive development of sport and encourage the participation of the population in the practice and organization of physical and sport activities.

4.3. Appropriate structures must be established for the training of personnel for physical education and sport. Personnel who have received such training must be given a status in keeping with the duties they perform.

Article 5. Adequate facilities and equipment are essential to physical education and sport

5.1. Adequate and sufficient facilities and equipment most be provided and installed to meet the needs of intensive and safe participation in both in-school and out-of-school programmes concerning physical education and sport.

5.2. It is incumbent on governments, public authorities, schools and appropriate private agencies, at all levels to join forces and plan together so as to provide and make optimum use of installations, facilities and equipment for physical education and sport.

5.3. It is essential that plans for rural and urban development include provision for longterm needs in the matter of installations, facilities and equipment for physical education and sport, taking into account the opportunities offered by the natural environment.

Article 6. Research and evaluation are indispensable components of the development of physical education and sport

6.1. Research and evaluation in physical education and sport should make for the progress of all forms of sport and help to bring about an improvement in the health and safety of participants as well as in training methods and organization and management procedures. The education system will thereby benefit from innovations calculated to develop better teaching methods and standards of performance.

6.2. Scientific research, whose social implications in this sphere should not be overlooked, must be oriented in such a way that it does not allow of improper applications to Physical education and sport.

Article 7. Protection of the ethical and moral values of physical education and sport must be a constant concern for all

7.1. Top-class sport and sport practised by all must be protected against any abuse. The serious dangers with which phenomena such as violence, doping and commercial excesses threaten its moral values, image and prestige pervert its very nature and change its educative and health promoting function. The public authorities, voluntary sports associations, specialized non-governmental organizations, the Olympic Movement, educators, parents, supporters' clubs, trainers, sports managers and the athletes themselves must combine their efforts in order to eliminate these evils. The media have a special role to play, in keeping with Article 8 in supporting and disseminating information about these efforts.

7.2. A prominent place must be assigned in curricula to educational activities based on the values of sport and the consequences of the interactions between sport, society and culture.

7.3. It is important that all sports authorities and sportsmen and women be conscious of the risks to athletes, and more especially to children, of precocious and inappropriate training and psychological pressures of every kind.

7.4. No effort must be spared to highlight the harmful affects of doping, which is both injurious to health and contrary to the sporting ethic, or to protect the physical and mental health of athletes, the virtues of fair play and competition, the integrity of the sporting community and the rights of people participating in it at any level whatsoever. It is crucial that the fight against doping should win the support of national and international authorities at various levels, and of parents, educators, the medical profession, the media, trainers, sports managers, and the athletes themselves, to ensure that they abide by the principles set out in the existing texts, and more particularly the International Olympic Charter against Doping in Sport. To that end, a harmonized and concerted policy must guide them in the preparation and application of anti-doping measures and of the educational action to be undertaken.

Article 8. Information and documentation help to promote physical education and sport

8.1. The collection, provision and dissemination of information and documentation on physical education and sport constitute a major necessity. In particular, there is a need to circulate information on the results of research and evaluation studies concerning programmes, experiments and activities.

Article 9. The mass media should exert a positive influence on physical education and sport

9.1. Without prejudice to the right of freedom of information, it is essential that everyone involved in the mass media be fully conscious of his responsibilities having regard to the social importance, the humanistic purpose and the moral values embodied in physical education and sport.

9.2. Relations between those involved in the mass media and specialists in physical education and sport must be close and based on mutual confidence in order and sport and to ensure objective and well-founded information. Training of personnel for the media may include elements relating to physical education and sport.

Article 10. National institutions play a major role in physical education and sport

10.1. It is essential that public authorities at all levels and specialized non-governmental bodies encourage those physical education and sport activities whose educational value is most evident. Their action shall consist in enforcing legislation and regulations, providing material assistance and adopting all other measures of encouragement. stimulation and control. The public authorities will also ensure that such fiscal measures are adopted as may encourage these activities.

10.2. It is incumbent on all institutions responsible for physical education .and sport to promote a consistent, overall and decentralized plan of action in the framework of lifelong education so as to allow for continuity and co-ordination between compulsory physical activities and those practised freely and spontaneously.

Article 11. International co-operation is a prerequisite for the universal and well-balanced promotion of physical education and sport

11.1. It is essential that States and those international and regional intergovernmental and non-governmental organizations in which interested countries are represented and which are responsible for physical education and sport give physical education and sport greater prominence in international bilateral and multilateral co-operation.

11.2. International co-operation must be prompted by wholly disinterested motives in order to promote and stimulate endogenous development in this field.

11.3. Through co-operation and the pursuit of mutual interests in the universal language of physical education and sport, all peoples will contribute to the preservation of lasting peace, mutual respect and friendship and will thus create a propitious climate for solving international problems. Close collaboration between all interested national and international governmental and non-governmental agencies, based on respect for the specific competence of each, will necessarily encourage the development of physical education and sport throughout the world.

6

Challenges of Physical Education

Gender Equity Issues and Challenges in Physical Education and Sports

The participation of females in physical activity and sport declines at a very young age. Fewer school sports and activities are offered to girls; teams are mainly segregated; opportunities are limited. Boys' teams tend to command the use of facilities. Rules and conventional practices in sport favour the physical strength and development of boys. Sport and physical activity is based on decades of traditions and practices which favour male participation.

Involvement in physical activity and sport is extremely important to girls and women. A decline in involvement may result in a reduced fitness level over the life cycle (absence of strength, poorer cardiovascular levels, diminishing bone density, a poor sense of body image, and low self-esteem). Lack of physical strength increases women's vulnerability in an era of violence. Loss of opportunity to enjoy the sheer pleasure of the sport experience is problem enough.

Our society has expectations about appropriate behaviours, attitudes, beliefs and values for males and females. Socialization - the teaching of gender roles - is performed by many agencies in society: family, school, community, religious institutions, media and peer group. The socialization process by which individuals learn gender roles is lifelong, although the early years are very formative. The resulting sex-role stereotyping has a profound impact on female participation in, and attitudes toward, physical activity and sport:

— Girls are generally expected to be gentle, non-assertive and dependent; boys are expected to be boisterous, aggressive and independent. In families and schools, boys and girls are rewarded for gender behaviour which is considered appropriate and discouraged or punished for behaviour which is not considered appropriate.

— Females are accorded status and peer recognition on the basis of good looks and attractive clothes. Expectations about female body image include strong disapproval of muscular or "mannish" females. While being fit is increasingly valued for females, it is still important to "look nice". Males learn to be proud of having strong and powerful bodies, and females still learn to undervalue these qualities in themselves.

— Stereotypical notions of female abilities underlie traditional beliefs that women do not possess the personality characteristics required to be successful coaches or officials regardless of their qualifications.

— Socialized attitudes are reinforced by inequity in early experiences of physical activity and sport. Girls are less likely than boys to be given adequate coaching in sport, to be exposed to a wide variety of sport experiences in their youth, or to have highly visible role models.

In general, physical activity and sport are highly valued for males and not for females. Being good at sports is an attribute which is highly ranked for males by males, and for males by females. It is ranked very low for females by both females and males. For females, sport and physical activity are often treated as distractions from other goals in life, rather than fundamental to living a healthy life.

School environments are a significant factor in the absence of the physical activity and sport experience and its myriad health, happiness, and protection benefits in the lives of many women. The first step in dealing with the issue of gender equity is to recognize that inequity exists.

Challenges and Responses

The following challenges and responses highlight some of these notions and provide background information for discussion.

Challenges:

— Girls are more easily injured than boys in physical activity.

— Girls' muscles are weaker than boys.

— Both girls and boys are treated equally in physical education and sport.

— Girls should avoid vigorous activity while menstruating.

— Special measures and equity programs don't promote females based on individual merit but on gender. This undermines women and the confidence of males in female abilities.

— Females choose to participate less in sport; they're less interested; they're not interested in developing their skills.

— Doesn't a plan of action to achieve gender equity lead to reverse discrimination? That's certainly not fair!

Responses:

— The well conditioned female is not more susceptible to injury than the well conditioned male.

— Muscles of the same size have the same strength whether they are in girls or boys. Making adjustments for body size differences will show that trained girls can generate as much muscular power as trained boys.

— Most educators and coaches believe that they treat people fairly and equally. However, the principle of equal treatment tends to ignore the fact that girls and boys differ in their interests, resources and previous experiences. To treat them equally ignores their individuality and limits the extent to which educators value their individual backgrounds, interests and abilities.

Furthermore, in actual practice, treating students equally is simply not possible. No effective teacher treats all students in a mixed ability class the same. Classroom interaction studies show that teachers consistently give more attention to boys than to girls in co-educational settings, that their judgement of the same behaviour when displayed by boys and girls differs, and that interaction between teachers and students is affected by factors of ethnicity, social class, and age.

Studies have shown that routine exercise may be helpful in the prevention of painful and irregular menstrual cycles. Because of the patriarchal nature of the system it is difficult for most females to make it in sport on their own merit. In addition, the progress females have made in sport has often shown that one woman on her own can't change the system. The problem is bigger than one person; it's not a problem of individual merit. Policies and systems need to be in place to change this.

If you examine inequality and ask girls and women for their explanations of the different levels of participation in sport, you'll begin to see another picture. The combination of discriminatory practices in physical activity and sport and women's position in society as a whole means that females are disadvantaged in the sport system. Gender equity means equal access to participation in physical activity and sport and to positions of responsibility in sport organizations. That doesn't exist today. An equity plan introduces positive guidelines to help make systems and procedures more fair.

In the past the curriculum has perpetuated race, class, gender and ethnic divisions and has emphasized separateness, rather than common citizenship and nationhood. It was therefore imperative that the curriculum be restructured to reflect the values and principals of our new democratic society.

The lack of support and facilitation in sports participation for young females has been well documented. Adolescent females who tend to reject physical activity and school physical education (PE) are unable to reap the psychological benefits, such as increased self-confidence, which participation could evoke. At a time when heightened awareness of physical and cognitive changes particularly in relation to others, can often become manifested in self-effacing behaviour and low self-esteem, this rejection is of particular concern.

Burden of Physical Inactivity and Poor Nutrition

The importance of proper nutrition and physical activity in reducing rates of disease and death from chronic diseases has been well established. Poor diet and physical inactivity cause 310,000 to 580,000 deaths per year and are major contributors to disabilities that result from diabetes, osteoporosis, obesity, and stroke.

The results of one study showed that 14% of all U.S. deaths in 1990 could be attributed to poor diet and activity patterns, and another study linked sedentary lifestyles to 23% of chronic disease-related deaths in the United States in 1986. According to *Healthy People 2010*, about 75% of Americans do not eat enough fruit, more than half do not eat enough vegetables, and 64% consume too much saturated fat. The diets of many population subgroups contain too much total fat, saturated fat, and calories but not enough of other important elements such as calcium. Low fruit and vegetable consumption and high saturated fat intake are associated with coronary heart disease, some cancers, and diabetes.

Regular physical activity is essential for a healthy life. Physically inactive people are almost twice as likely to develop coronary heart disease as people who engage in regular physical activity. Thus physical inactivity poses almost as much risk for heart disease as cigarette smoking, high blood pressure, or a high cholesterol level, but is more prevalent than any of these other risk factors. People with other risk factors for coronary heart disease, such as obesity and hypertension, may particularly benefit from physical activity. It also helps older adults remain independent and enhances the quality of life for people of all ages.

Obesity or overweight status is defined by body mass index (BMI), which is derived by dividing weight in kilograms by the square of height in meters. From 1991-2000, the prevalence of obesity (defined as BMI > 30 k/m^2) among adults increased nationally, in every state, and in all segments of the population. Obesity leads to numerous health problems, including hypertension, dyslipidemia, type 2 diabetes, coronary heart disease, stroke, gall bladder disease, osteoarthritis, sleep apnea, respiratory problems, and some cancers (e.g., endometrial, breast, prostate, and colon cancers). Because obesity is a risk factor for several chronic diseases, the economic and social consequences of this obesity epidemic could be overwhelming.

While many factors have contributed to the obesity epidemic, prevention efforts should focus on helping people reduce their calorie intake and increase their physical activity. The prevalence of obesity is increasing more rapidly among children than among adults. Because a growing body of evidence suggests that breastfeeding offers protection against excessive weight gain in childhood and adolescence, CDC advocates breastfeeding as a reasonable strategy for reducing children's risk of becoming overweight.

The economic burden of poor diet, physical inactivity, and obesity is substantial. All are significant risk factors for developing coronary heart disease, certain types of cancer, stroke, and diabetes, conditions that involve considerable medical expense as well as lost work time, disability, and premature death. In one study, the direct medical cost for dietrelated manifestations of these four conditions was estimated at $33.6 billion (in 1995 dollars) and the total cost, including lost productivity because of illness and premature death, was estimated to be $70.9 billion. In another study based on 1987 medical expenditure data, researchers estimated that if the more than 88 million inactive Americans over the age of 15 began engaging in regular moderate physical activity, annual national medical costs could be reduced by as much as $76.6 billion in 2000 dollars.

The medical costs associated with obesity are even higher: an estimated $100 billion annually based on 1995 data. Taken together, inactivity and obesity accounted for 9.4% of the 1995 health care expenditures in the United States. In addition to these economic costs, immeasurable costs due to social and emotional problems, both for those affected and for their friends and families, may result from inactivity- and obesity-related diseases.

The problems associated with poor diet, physical inactivity, and obesity affect most population segments; however, there are marked disparities in the impact that these problems have on various groups of people, particularly by race/ethnicity and by education level.

The subject "Physical Education and Health" has a broad perspective of health. Students are to acquire increased knowledge of how their own body functions and how healthy food habits, regular physical activities, and outdoor life can improve their physical and mental well-being. Through their own practice and experiences, students are to develop the desire and will to partake in physical activities. The course is to lead to students finding different ways of conducting individual physical training, and developing and strengthening their health, both whilst at school, and later during further studies and working life.

Thus, the education aims at students becoming more conscious of health and environment, and having a greater opportunity to participate actively in working with questions concerning health, at work and in society as a whole. Health is a whole, consisting of physical, mental and social well-being, which can lead to a better quality of life. Participation in sports influences health by training and developing the body. By education students are to become more conscious of the importance of their own lifestyles in respect of health and environment, and to develop an awareness of their bodies, and a positive self image.

Students are to gain increased knowledge about food, exercise and ergonomics as well as the harmful effects of drugs and doping. The course is to provide opportunities to experience outdoor life and nature, thereby contributing to students developing an ecologically sound basic view of, and the will to take greater responsibility for, our common environment. The education provided is to take into consideration the differing individual conditions of students, and pay attention to differences between sexes as well as individuals.

Students are to broaden their knowledge in the areas of sport and health, and gain the knowledge needed to be able to reflect independently over, and analyse ways and methods of, achieving health and well-being, both from an individual viewpoint as well as that of a civic perspective. On completion of the course students will:

— be aware and have experience of the physiological and psychological effects of different kinds of physical training;

— be able to perform, and both independently and as a member of a team to organise, carry out and evaluate some kind of sports activity;

— have increased their knowledge of and skill in sports activities of significance in Swedish culture; have participated in and increased their knowledge of outdoor activities;

— be aware of basic ecological factors in different natural environments;

— be familiar with the safety aspects associated with different kinds of outdoor activity;

— have thorough knowledge of health problems which are a burden to society, and to know of different suggestions for their solution;

— know how to deal with and combat harmful stress;

— be able to analyse the effect on health of different kinds of working environment;

— be able to discuss, from a historical angle, the connection between environment and human health.

The Third World, particularly India, has been drugged by globalisation as a panacea (or placebo?) for its developmental problems while two other opiates, viz., privatisation and liberalisation have received a pejorative slant from progressive economists. This trinity of mantras, minted abroad and imposed on India is the economic narcotic of the Indian elite. But another psychotropic addiction, far more devastating and dementing and desperado-spawning, is the sinister spread of narco- terrorism, drug trafficking and other incalculable vices which have gained international currency among terrorists, achieved irresistible popularity among adolescent and adult victims of both sexes, and criminalised the rich and the poor alike, corrupting a whole generation beyond redemption.

The drug empire is so powerful that the police, courts and prisons are no match for this grave menace. This globalisation process, too insidious and a money-minting business, with violent transnational networks, to be tracked down by the national police single-handed, too impregnably protected by underground mafia and dubious power-brokers, that health, peace and security of people everywhere are in perennial peril.

Necessarily, human survival drives nations, whatever their ideological and other antagonisms be, to come together for collective policing, jointly evolving operational strategies of detection and destruction of production, distribution and consumption of narcotics and psychotropics unlimited and for deterrent as well as rehabilitative criminal justice on a cooperative basis worldwide. Every country has stakes in the extirpation of this trade in chemically-catalysed insanity. Confronted by this challenge, the United Nations has swung into action, set up an international drug control programme and is mobilising world opinion and action with an Agenda of Operation Global Drug Eradication. A vision of a new drug-free world human order is a consummation worth any sacrifice. Such a transformation will spell abatement of desperate terrorism, violent crime, psychic collapse, broken homes, ubiquitous corruption and cultural decline of the younger generation. Drug abuse and drug-related crimes are escalating and this mafiasque trend is pathologically pervasive, disregarding national barriers.

The Lakshmibai National College (now Institute) of Physical Education was established by Government of India, on 17th August, 1957, the centenary year of the first war of Independence. The Institute is located at Gwalior where Rani Lakshmibai of Jhansi had lost her life. In recognistion of the educational services rendered by the Institute in the field of physical education, sports and research and on the recommendations of the University Grants Commission, the Government of India, Ministry of Human Resource Development (Department of Education) declared this Institute as a "Deemed to be a University".

Main Schemes for Sports Authority of India

The main programmes and activities of SAI consist of schemes drawn up and approved within the SAI and schemes of the Department implemented through the SAI on an agency basis. The main schemes of the SAI are given below:

— National Sports Talent Contest (NSTC)

— Special Area Games

— Sports Projects Development Area (SPDA)

— Sports Hostel Scheme

— Boys Sports Companies in the Army

— National Coaching Scheme

— Sports Science Research Fellowship Scheme

(a) National Sports Talent Contest (NSTC)

Started in 1985, this scheme attempts to identify talented school children in the age group of 9 to 12 years. Children are selected in 10 Olympic disciplines, viz. Athletics, Basketball, Badminton, Boxing, Football, Gymnastics, Hockey, Table Tennis, Volleyball and Wrestling through a series of tests and contests held at various levels.

Following selection, these children are admitted in SAI adopted schools (of which there are 58 at present) where their board, lodging and tuition fees are met by SAI. SAI also provides coaches and special infrastructure facilities to these schools, along with recurring grants for maintenance and equipment.

(b) Special Area Games

This scheme, started in 1985, aims at identifying population groups and regions where natural talent and aptitude for a particular sport exists. The scheme involves a process of identification and survey of areas and regions, special competitions to assess potential, selection of promising young boys and girls and intensive training at SAG centres, where educational and vocational training facilities are also provided.

(c) Sports Projects Development Area (SPDA)

This Scheme, started in 1988, aims at providing basic sports facilities at 78 locations throughout the country, where a comprehensive and integrated system of coaching and training is provided to talented young sportspersons in the age group of 9 to 14 years. This is aimed at providing in-house facilities to the talented youth in their own states. A maximum of three Olympic disciplines, in addition to one indigenous game, are offered for training. Three Olympic disciplines should generally include at least one of the three mother disciplines, i.e. athletics, gymnastics, swimming in each centre. Thirty out of 34 SPDA Centres have started functioning, with a total strength of 679 sportspersons. An amount of Rs. 1.00 crore is budgeted for the construction of these Centres (met equally by the Centre and the concerned State), and all running costs are met by SAI.

(d) Sports Hostel Scheme

This Scheme was introduced to provide basic facilities in each State and National level Championships. All running costs, including equipment, training, etc. are provided by SAI. Each hostel has a sanctioned strength of 50 boys and 30 girls. 18 hostels have so far been established with 895 children.

(e) Boys Sports Companies in the Army

This scheme is an extension of the N.S.T.C. scheme and was approved for implementation from the year 1991-92. SAI and Army authorities have jointly launched this Scheme to scout talented boys upto the age of 14 years from rural, semi urban and tribal areas and train them in sports.

Seventeen Boys Sports Companies for 2000 boys are to be set up during the VIII Plan at selected Regimental Centres. The boys will be put into Regimental Schools which will be affiliated to the CBSE. On attaining the age of 17 years and on completion of 10th standard, the boys will be absorbed in the Army, if they so wish. Thereby, a job is guaranteed to them. The running costs are borne by SAI. It also provides a one time grant to the Army for creation and development of sports infrastructure, purchase of essential sports equipment upto Rs. 3.00 Iakh and for training kit/aid upto Rs.1.00 lakh. Thereafter, an annual grant of Rs. 50,000/ is provided. 17 Boys Sports

Companies have become functional with a total strength of 859 sportspersons.

(f) National Coaching Scheme

The National Coaching Scheme, which was first introduced in 1955, is meant to encourage people to take up coaching. The Scheme, over the years has undergone numerous changes and is now a major source for meeting the requirement of coaches by various user agencies.

Under the Scheme, coaches are made available to States/ UTs for State coaching centres, district coaching and university field stations and also to national sports federations/ associations. Coaches are also deployed in SAI regional centres, academic wings and in house training centres. At present, the total strength of coaches under the scheme is 1677.

(g) Sports Science Research Fellowship Scheme

The Sports Authority of India awards Sports Science Fellowships to research workers for carrying out research in sports science related areas such as sports physiology, sports injuries, sports big mechanics and training methods. Under the Scheme, 5-10 fellowships are awarded every year. The value of each fellowship grant is Rs. 20,000/ per annum with an additional contingency grant of Rs. 10,000/ per annum Academic Wings.

The Sports Authority of India has two functional wings relating to academics which are in the fields of sports and physical education. These are:

(a) Netaji Subhas National Institute of Sports, Patiala (NSNIS)

The Institute conducts academic courses for training of coaches and looks after research and development in sports related subjects. It conducts 24 months' diploma courses in fifteen sports disciplines and also offers 22 months' specialised post diploma master's course and 1 year post graduate diploma course in sports medicine. NSNIS is the only institute of its kind in the country and has so far trained 11,751 coaches at Patiala and at its centres at Bangalore (established in 1975), Calcutta (1983) and Gandhinagar (1987). In addition, under the Mass Sports Participation Programme, certificate courses of six weeks duration were held at these centres and 15,601 sports instructors have so far been trained. NSNIS is also conducting one year post MBBS Diploma course in sports medicine and 28 doctors have so far qualified. The period of this course has been raised to two year from the academic session 1993- 94.

(b) LNCPE, Trivandrum

This college was inaugurated in 1984 and is fast developing in terms of infrastructural facilities, academic programmes and other essential requirements. This college offers a 3 year Bachelor of Physical Education (BPE) and 2 years M.PE degree courses. One hundred and forty six students (67 boys and 59 girls) are at present studying in the college. Upto the academic year 1995-96, 270 students have passed out from the college.

Moving into the Future

Physical activity is critical to the development and maintenance of good health. The goal of physical education is to develop physically educated individuals who have the knowledge, skills, and confidence to enjoy a lifetime of healthful physical activity.

A physically educated person:

Standard 1: Demonstrates competency in motor skills and movement patterns needed to perform a variety of physical activities.

Standard 2: Demonstrates understanding of movement concepts, principles, strategies, and tactics as they apply to the learning and performance of physical activities.

Standard 3: Participates regularly in physical activity.

Standard 4: Achieves and maintains a health-enhancing level of physical fitness.

Standard 5: Exhibits responsible personal and social behavior that respects self and others in physical activity settings.

Standard 6: Values physical activity for health, enjoyment, challenge, self-expression, and/or social interaction.

What is worth teaching and learning in physical education? The national content standards define what a student should know and be able to do as result of a quality physical education program. They provide a framework for developing realistic and achievable expectations for student performance at every grade level. These expectations are the first step in designing an instructionally aligned program.

States and local school districts across the country have used the national standards to develop standards, frameworks, and curricula. Others have revised their existing standards and curricula to align with the national standards. The national standards demonstrate that physical education has academic standing equal to other subject areas. They describe achievement, show that knowledge and skills matter, and confirm that mere willing participation is not the same as education. In short, national physical education standards bring accountability and rigor to the profession.

As teachers in England and Wales once again face the prospect of responding to a revision of the National Curriculum for Physical Education (NCPE). In his recent work The Curriculum of the Future, Young (1998) draws attention to the changing organisation of work and changing characteristics of economic development.

Specifically, he sees societies moving towards 'human resource-led economic growth', in which 'it is national systems of education and training rather than national economies that will determine the fate of nations'. In Young's view these changes raise fundamental questions about the current design of curricula, their inherent specialisms and divisions. He calls for new 'connective specialisms' to be developed, in which subject communities actively address and respond to the changing world of work, move beyond a view of subjects as 'ends in themselves' and address the complex contexts in which the knowledge to which they give access might be applied.

While certainly supporting Young's stance, educators point to a need to respond not only to the changing world of work, but to changes in all arenas of the societies in which they live and work. Arguably, the changing leisure activities, changing relationships between work and leisure, and changing relationships between individuals, should be as much a concern for educational planners as the changing world of work. Furthermore, they stress the need to move from a view of education responding, or needing to respond to such changes, to a view of it as a force for future changes. Thus, in considering new 'connective specialisms' they should be contemplating what worlds of work and leisure, and what societies they are seeking connections to.

In the context of transformation of curricula, transformations of and in society should not be overlooked. Young emphasises that '... curriculum debates, implicitly or explicitly, are always debates about alternative views of society and its future'. Furthermore, the dynamic between curricula and society is the very basis of our potential to be proactive rather than merely reactive in social change. Educators need to remember that futures have to be made, they do not just happen'. Thus, in considering contemporary curricula, Young highlights the need to consider the extent to which these represent 'a future society that they can endorse or a past society that they want to change'.

Does physical education contribute to the development of societies that we endorse? With changes in societies, and our visions for the future, is there a need for changes in our specialism? How can physical education be, in Young's terms, 'more connective' (within the subject,.with other aspects of the curriculum, and with lives and societies beyond schools) and express a 'lifetime approach' to education?

If visions are to be realised, what approaches and skills do teachers need to develop, what relations do they need to facilitate with pupils, amongst pupils, with colleagues, with parents and with individuals from other organisations involved in the provision of physical education and sport for young people? Certainly, these are challenging issues for the profession to address, but also issues about which discussion seems long overdue. At this point educators will be quite open about their own visions and agendas.

In education and in physical education specifically, educators are seeking curricula and pedagogical practices that are directed towards the development of critically informed citizens who are committed to playing a part in establishing more equitable societies in which all individuals are valued; in which individual, social and cultural differences are celebrated as a richness of society; and in which knowledge is something to be collectively, collaboratively and creatively advanced, rather than pre-defined and 'delivered'.

Physical education can play a key role in such developments. In particular they see it as having great potential to facilitate self-directed and self-inspired learning, and to provide contexts and experiences that demonstrate the importance and value of collective as well as individual agendas and actions. As a subject and a profession, physical education can take a lead in designing and developing an education 'for a world of rapid change in which both flexible attitudes and enduring values have a part to play'. However, they also believe that the realisation of such visions demands radical changes in and of physical education in all arenas, and specifically, in policy, in curriculum design and in lesson contexts.

In Bernstein's terms, emphasise the need for a curriculum structure that signals a very different 'voice' in physical education and that clearly prompts and supports the development of different 'messages' . A need for a weakening of both the classification and framing of physical education curricula, characterised by an emphasis on the connective and collective value of different contexts of learning, and a shift from an emphasis on teaching pre-defined knowledge, skills and understanding, towards notions of the teacher as a facilitator of learning in a negotiated curriculumthat seeks to address the individual needs and interests of all pupils, while also reflecting and pursuing collective interests and values.

For those readers unfamiliar with Bernstein's concepts, Bernstein explains that the form and strength of categories of knowledge provide curricula with a specific emphasis, orientation or 'voice'. Curriculum knowledge can be regarded as shaped and defined by categories (subjects, or in the specific context of physical education, often activities) and the relations between them. The curricula then developed within the context of particular categories represent the realised form of the voice, or the 'message'.

Different voices (i.e. different forms of categorisation in and of curricula) signify the privileging of different knowledge. Bernstein emphasises that the key consideration in addressing the potential for the creation of a new voice is the strength of classification (degree of insulation between categories) inherent in curricula. Reducing insulation is fundamental to changing the principle of classification and thereby privileging new or different knowledge in education.

If they are also concerned with the matters of who plays what role in the creation of knowledge, and the pedagogical practices that will feature in schools, they also need to consider the strength of framing (referring to relationships between individuals) that is promoted by the particular 'voice' of curricula and that feature in the 'messages' arising. There are different types of learning and different types of learners, changes in the roles and relationships of teachers and pupils seem particularly important.

Bernstein's work a need for:

- a change in the principle of classification of physical education curricula;
- a weakening of that classification and weaker framing in physical education;
- a new voice to be established for the curriculum; and
- the development of new messages in teaching.

The Aims and Claims of Physical Education

Over the years many within the profession have drawn attention to the inaccuracies inherent in both public and political perceptions of what physical education 'is' and 'is about'. Specifically, statements have been made that have sought to clarify that physical education is not merely about 'doing', nor can it be equated with 'sport'. For example, the non-statutory guidance issued to accompany the 1992 National Curriculum for Physical Education in England and Wales highlighted that:

> In physical education the emphasis is on learning in a mainly physical context. The purpose of the learning is to develop specific knowledge, skills and understanding and to promote physical development and competence. The learning promotes participation in sport while Sport is the term applied to a range of physical activities where emphasis is on participation and competition. Different sporting activities can and do contribute to learning.

However, while physical educationalists may be in agreement about what the subject 'is not', the matter of what the core aims of the subject are remains far less clear and a source of apparent tension. Claims about the contribution of the subject to children's development, later lives and to society are multiple and diverse.

For example, the mission statement of the Physical Education Association of the United Kingdom (PEAUK) states that physical education enables young people to develop an appreciation of skilful performance', that it 'aids the development of healthy lifestyles' and that it 'contributes to the spiritual, moral, social and cultural awareness of young people'. Meanwhile, the British Association of Advisers and Lecturers in Physical Education (BAALPE) has stated that 'It remains critical to the well-being of every child and the Nation's health generally, that there is an entitlement to a rigorous physical education programme'.

Sir Rodney Walker, the Chairman of the English Sports Council, has stressed that 'The contribution of the PE curriculum to a child's education and as an integral element of Sport for All at grass roots level should not be underestimated'. Physical education can legitimately continue to make varied claims and pursue multiple agendas. Debate about both the compatibility of these multiple claims and their implications for the content and structure of curricula seems to have been largely overlooked in contemporary times. As Armour and Jones have suggested, 'physical education may be trying to do too much'. They suggest that it may have '... failed to identify a specific focus within its huge potential'.

Perhaps the critical failure is that the implications of the various aims for curriculum design, teaching and learning, have been inadequately explored, and furthermore, in the absence of such inquiry, educators have witnessed the emergence of a particular dominant form and focus. The form and focus that they refer to has become established to the point that it has attained the status of being 'the obvious' and for many people (most notably, members of the public and politicians, but surely also many within the profession itself), the only possible structure and orientation for the subject.

Goodson likened the making of the curriculum to 'the notion of trying to sell refrigerators to the eskimos ... Nobody asks the question of why refrigerators, of how such an inappropriate product came to be at the centre of the action'. What they are referring to, of course, is the focus upon the learning of activities (and sports) and the fact that whatever sets of interests physical education has claimed to serve, its curricula have remained remarkably unchanged in form.

Prior to and throughout the development of the National Curriculum for Physical Education, the form of most physical education curricula has given every appearance of legitimating a view of physical education as comprising merely a collection of activities. Educators acknowledge that this is by no means a characteristic unique to physical education in England and Wales, and indeed, stress that the matters they raise are ones of international relevance.

Thus, central to the notion of a 'new specialism' with the capacity to facilitate realisation of the aims for learning and for learners in physical education is a fundamental restructuring of the subject that will signal a redefinition of the subject and that will demand quite radical reform of curricula associated with it. In these terms, they have some sympathies with Locke's reflection that 'If physical education is to have a significant presence in the secondary schools of the 21st century, it is better to chuck the dominant model ... and start over from scratch'. However, the reality in all arenas of policy and curriculum development is that they are not 'starting from scratch', that they cannot and should not deny the rich history of physical education, and that they need to be taking due account of, be building upon, and relating to, established practices.

From Critical Pedagogy to CurriculumFramework

Throughout the development of the NCPE in England and Wales there has been very limited opportunity for any review of the underlying structure and framework of the subject. Activities, or areas of activity have retained a privileged position in the framework, in the requirements for teaching and learning, and in the curricula developed in response to these requirements.

With activity based divisions, and a continuing emphasis of the differences between various areas of activity, the curriculum does not encourage a focus upon connective aspects or potential of the subject; that is, connections in the learning that may occur in different activity contexts; connections between learning in physical education and learning in other curriculum areas; and between learning in physical education and experiences and learning beyond schools.

Currently the statutory order for the NCPE, and many curricula arising from those requirements, display strong classification and insulation in relation to both the subject of physical education as a whole and what are then defined as its component parts. Regrettably, in their view, the latest revision of the NCPE may do little to counter this emphasis. A document recently issued by the *Qualifications and Curriculum Authority* (QCA) that is explicitly designed to provide clarity and 'uniformity' in interpretations of particular terminology has highlighted the continued tendency to portray various areas of activity as distinct from one another, and to identify them as mechanisms for promoting different values and interests.

To develop as a connective specialism and to establish a focus upon the contribution that physical education can make to the whole curriculum, and to the whole education of children, like Locke they question whether a solution can be found by alterations to one or more of the established parts, or rather, whether whole-scale change is what is required. Macdonald & Brooker agree that the subject 'needs to be conceptualised as an educational process, positioned within educational discourses and drawing upon educational argument'.

To achieve this, a need for physical education to clearly articulate its purposes in relation to visions of and for future citizens and societies, to identify the kind of knowledge, skills and understanding that underpin the realisation of those visions, and to establish these as the core learning towards which teaching is explicitly directed. The contribution to learning that they see the subject as providing, rather than the activities through which they may ultimately achieve that contribution, should become the explicit defining feature of the subject, and should provide the framework for curriculum development. Therefore, educators see a need for a thematically oriented, rather than activity-based curriculum, and a framework that openly privileges what they may term 'themes' or 'strands of learning'. Such an approach would emphasise the way in which collectively various activities (or areas of activity) may facilitate and further particular learning. It would provide a direct challenge to the current insulation and strong classifi cation inherent in physical education curricula and specifically, in the statutory texts of the NCPE. As indicated above, for Bernstein, reducing the degree of insulation between categories is fundamental to establishing a new voice in curricula.

Turning to the specifics of structure and organisation of the curriculum, they are looking for a move away from teaching units or lessons defined in terms of an activity (for example, football or gymnastics). Instead, they envisage themes that represent the identified 'core learning' as defining units of work, and an activity or combination of activities then providing the medium and contexts for the learning that has been established as the focus for the unit, and that relates explicitly to the particular theme. The critical points to note are that the dominant focus is the specified core learning for physical education and that this is not defined in terms of specific activities or sports, but rather, in terms of themes.

The basis for the categorisation of physical education curricula is different to that currently so firmly established in their subject. The proposed structure therefore signifies the promotion of a different voice for the curriculumand reflects Crum's view that 'the essence of physical education is not "learning to move" but "moving to learn". While emphasising this distinct shift in the focus and organisation of curricula, educators stress that their proposed approach certainly does not preclude the development of skills, knowledge and understanding associated with specific activities or sports.

To the contrary, they would expect that such learning would be notably advanced by the learning focus and experiences provided in physical education and articulated in the themes (or strands of learning) established for the subject. They anticipate that curricula will therefore be explicitly concerned with matters that are fundamental to the development of participation and performance in physical activity and sport, and that physical education will thereby play a key (and perhaps far more effective) role in enabling, encouraging and extending participation and performance.

They appreciate the difficulty of trying to envisage the implementation of what may seem rather vague ideas and the need to therefore substantiate their discussion with some further detail of the curriculum developments that they are proposing. The latest revision of the NCPE in England can be regarded as taking a step that quite openly seeks to clarify the focus of teaching and learning in physical education. Specifically, it is proposed that 'core strands of learning' will be established and these are currently identified as:

- acquiring and developing skills
- applying and combining
- improving and evaluating performance
- Knowledge and understanding of fitness and health.

Regrettably, in the context (and particularly timescale) of this revision of the NCPE, there has not been the scope, nor opportunity to debate whether these are the desirable or appropriate strands of learning for physical education in the 21st century. Furthermore, and arguably of greater significance, is the fact that while establishing these strands, the proposals have retained a structure in which areas of activity are the focus for outline of the programmes of study in physical education.

In retaining this characteristic the proposals appear to display and promote strong classification and insulation in prospective curricula. In their view this focus on areas of activity rather than the newly created strands signifies a fundamental conceptual tension in the NCPE, and may prove a substantial barrier to attempts to develop 'new connectivity' in teaching and learning in physical education. Past research has highlighted the potential for new statutory requirements to be accommodated within largely unchanged units of work and patterns of teaching, and educators are inclined to question the degree to which the core strands identified will be foregrounded in teaching and learning in physical education.

In short, with the retention of the areas of activity they see every opportunity for the retention of organisational practices and foci that continue to legitimate the long established activity-based voice of physical education. In their view, if they are to see a new clarity of focus in teaching and learning in physical education, the programmes of study and the associated requirements for content coverage in curricula, and schemes of work arising in schools, must be (re-)defined in relation to the established strands.

The identification of appropriate (and feasible) activity contexts in which the programmes of study can be developed, then see the matters of flexibility in curricula design and the need for professional judgements coming to the fore, and where the new approaches to curriculum design will be needed if consistency between the voice and message of curricula (Bernstein, 1990, 1996; see also Penney, 1998a) is to be achieved. It is perhaps worth noting at this point that their suggestions for a thematic framework for curricula are not merely abstract, but rather, have important reference points. The 'history' of the particular suggestions demands some commentary. To a great extent, suggestions for and visions of 'an alternative' structure and emphasis have come from the realisation through comparative experiences of physical education, that 'there are alternatives' and alternative possibilities for the focus and structure of physical education.

Although often centring upon Health and Physical Education (HPE), rather than physical education, policy and curriculum developments in Australia have provided concrete contemporary examples of curriculum frameworks that present a notable contrast to activity-based models. In the national text for health and physical education, the strands of 'human functioning and physical activity', 'community structures and practices' and 'communication, investigation and application' are the suggested organisational framework for curricula, and those of 'human development', 'human movement', 'physical activity and the community', 'people and food', 'health of individuals and populations', 'safety' and 'human relations' provide the suggested framework for assessment.

Developments in Australia have certainly highlighted the challenges and also tensions arising in developing such proposals in school contexts, in which different boundaries and discourses may invariably be privileged in the organisational structure of the school if not the curriculum itself. In addition, however, these developments have prompted invaluable reflection amongst physical education communities in Australia and the initiation of some innovative curriculumdevelopments. It is direct experiences of such developments that has particularly drawn the attention to the potential for different learning priorities to come to the fore in physical education and the key role that curriculum frameworks may play in prompting such moves.

In addition, in proposing an alternative framework they were concerned to challenge what has appeared a key omission in the development of the new proposals for the National Curriculum for Physical Education in England. Teachers and others wishing to respond to these proposals have had no scope to consider whether the strands of learning proposed for the new NCPE in England are the most appropriate, or what alternatives they could consider. Proposing alternatives at this point in time seems critical to prompt such debate. The activity-based structure has never been a matter for discussion, so in the future development of the NCPE, these proposed strands may become a non-negotiable and fixed feature of the curriculum.

The themes that suggest that physical education curricula should adopt as an organisational framework and pedagogical focus are, therefore:

- movement and physical literacy;
- physical activity, health and fitness;
- competition and cooperation; and
- challenge.

In expanding briefly upon each of these themes emphasise the multidisciplinary nature of teaching and learning in physical education wish to see promoted in each theme. This as an important characteristic to be developed throughout physical education curricula, with reference therefore being made to physical, psychological, emotional and social dimensions of physical activity. All dimensions as requiring explicit reference in curricula if the aims and claims relating to these dimensions of learning are to be realised.

In addition, the curriculum structure should be such that particular units focus upon one theme, the need for curricula to be making connections between themes at appropriate points. Thus not only presenting a case for a new principle of classification but also, for curricula with weaker classification, so that links between different dimensions of the curriculum are promoted in teaching and learning. However, in relation to this and in other important respects, that are not presenting a fully developed model of 'an alternative curriculum'. A number of issues that demand thorough debate prior to proceeding to that level of detail, not least of which are:

- whether the themes that we have identified are regarded as an appropriate and adequate articulation of the breadth of learning that physical education is concerned to address;
- whether there should be consistency in the themes that define and structure the curriculum in primary and secondary school contexts, whether the themes should be different for the two sectors or whether different learning

priorities should be addressed via different 'weighting' of themes that are common to the two sectors; and

— precisely what we regard as desirable and feasible learning to address in and via physical education for each theme at different phases of education, and the progression in learning that we would therefore be seeking to facilitate.

All of these, suggest, are key points to be addressed in any further development of a curriculum model such as this. Furthermore, decisions on all are arguably an essential prerequisite to any further development of units or lessons that may feature within a thematically based curriculum.

There is a need to emphasise that the knowledge, skills and understanding that are not only physical in nature. The focus of attention is on physical development, but the complexity of that development is acknowledged. Thus, it is recognised that there are important psychological and sociological dimensions to physical development and that social and psychological skills and abilities required for this development, and for participation and performance in physical activities, need to be more explicit in curriculum design and teaching than may currently be the case.

While physical education may often claim to contribute to these dimensions of learning, it perhaps rarely facilitates or monitors this learning in a comprehensive or structured way. The collective as well as individual issues that are relevant here and that curricula need to engage with. As well as developing awareness of one's own body and its potential, we see physical education as having a role to play in instilling appreciation of the varied capacities of others in these terms.

Developing this focus in the curricula seems essential if they are to be effective in extending patterns of participation and performance in physical activity. With such extension in mind, educators should also recall their emphasis above of the 'wide array' of physical activities in modern society. They suggest that there is a need to review the precise nature of the skills, knowledge and understanding that are currently associated with movement and physical development, and moreover, the range of arenas that this aspect of physical education will thereby facilitate access to, or connections with.

Questions to consider are what skills, knowledge and understanding are being privileged and whether this is with particular patterns and arenas of physical activity in mind? Is there, for example, a tendency to be devoting attention to skills, knowledge and understanding that underpin participation and performance in team games and/or organised competitive sport, over and above giving due regard to that which is essential to the pursuit of more individually orientated participation in physical activity for the purposes of health and well-being? They are not suggesting that there are rigid boundaries in relation to the movement and physical development that they would regard as a foundation for engagement in different forms of physical activity for different purposes, but rather, they are stressing the need for the foundation to have sufficient breadth so as to maximise the scope of its potential application. They need a foundation that can facilitate multiple and diverse connections.

The second theme 'physical activity, health and fitness' centres upon the relationships between participation in physical activity and the health and well-being of individuals and societies. This theme therefore addresses the ways in which different physical activities can facilitate, but also in some forms and at some times may place at risk, physical, psychological and social well-being throughout one's life. It addresses, therefore, issues relevant to 'active futures' and lifelong interests in physical activity and health.

The theme also places individual participation and individual health and fitness in the context of societies and thus considers collective, not merely individual, agendas in relation to these matters. The inclusivity of provision and participation would be key issues to consider here, with curricula seeking to promote awareness and understanding of the different health needs and interests of individuals; help all pupils to develop patterns of engagement in physical activity that reflect their individual needs and interests in these terms; and consider the barriers that may currently be inhibiting the adoption of such behaviours.

Also emphasised here is a conceptualisation of health that encompasses cognitive as well as physical dimensions, and a conceptualisation of fitness that facilitates links with both sport and health. The focus is therefore upon '. fitness for life', with fitness for participation and performance in sport representing one aspect of a broader agenda to be addressed in teaching and learning, and cognitive as well as physical aspects of fitness being considered within this. In contemporary societies, as curriculum developments in Australia have particularly reflected, there seems a need for education to be concerned with pupils' current and future mental health, and for physical education to recognise and pursue the contribution that it may make in relation to this concern. They should perhaps be devoting more attention to the maintenance of mental health in and via various physical activities and therefore including experiences of, for example, martial arts in the curriculum.

'Competition and cooperation' is a theme that addresses what may regard as defining characteristics of participation and performance in a number of physical activities and particularly, in organised sports. A need for teaching and learning to focus upon the critical links between competition and cooperation rather than to mirror the tendency (certainly amongst the media and politicians) to regard them as diametrically opposed agendas in physical education. Thus, developing team work and 'fair play' would be foci in units associated with this theme and important potential for initiatives developed under the umbrella of 'Sport Education' and 'Teaching Games for Understanding' to inform the development of this theme.

The sport education model has usefully pointed to the valuable contribution that experiences in physical education make to a range of learning, and has arguably done much to promote and extend that range and encourage broader conceptualisations of 'skill development' and 'knowledge' relating to physical education. In addition, Sport Education points to the potential development of the 'negotiated curriculum' experiences referred to above, with students playing a more proactive role in defining these experiences and their own roles in them.

However, in this and in all of the themes, there is a need to retain a commitment to the contribution that a wide range of physical activities may make to teaching and learning. Therefore stress the need for competition and cooperation to be explored in and via a variety of contexts, and not only, for example, in and via team games. That other areas of activity, including individual as well as team activities, will be valuable in facilitating breadth of learning relating to competition and cooperation and that diversity in these respects can also serve to highlight relationships between individual and collective agendas.

In addition, they suggest that this may be an area in which there is a need for and/or potential benefit in extending the range of activities typically featuring in physical education curricula. In seeking to develop knowledge and understanding of competition and cooperation, it may be useful to include activities that pupils are less familiar with and that demand different patterns of play, communication and teamwork. Experience of a game such as chukeball could be a context in which these aspects of learning in physical education are notably extended.

The theme of 'challenge' may similarly be regarded as a defining characteristic of some physical activities, but also one that has perhaps been rather narrowly defined and explored in and via physical education. Again they return to the multidisciplinary nature of teaching and learning that they advocate. In this context, the need for physical educationalists to be addressing the psychological and social challenges, as well as the physical challenges, associated with and arising in contexts of participation and performance in physical activity.

With this broad perspective comes the potential linkage of the theme of challenge to a wide array of physical activities and environments. For example, learning experiences centring on dance would have as justifiable a place within a unit of work focusing on challenge as experiences of an activity such as rock climbing. Many pupils participating in a dance lesson may face notable personal challenges, the roots of which may well lie in social issues relating to body image and the gendered labelling of certain physical activities. The need for diversity in experiences and contexts if the multidisciplinary nature of the theme is to be articulated in teaching and learning.

Obviously, the precise nature of the contexts ultimately incorporated in a unit for this and indeed, any of the themes, would need to take due account of a number of issues, not least of which will be the physical resources, time and expertise on hand, but critically, also pupils' prior experiences and learning. Coherency and continuity must be a focus amidst diversity.

The different dimensions of 'challenge' that have pointed to could certainly be addressed within the context of a single area of activity. For example, while one dance lesson may specifically focus upon extending the physical demands, another lesson may be directed towards developing awareness and understanding of the inhibitions that some children and adults may experience in dance contexts.

Pedagogical Practices

A focus on the detail of teaching is certainly a critical dimension to consider, arguably the most significant, and one that others have highlighted as inadequately pursued in contemporary contexts of policy and curriculumdevelopment in physical education. In Bernstein's terms educators are specifically concerned with the capacity of the 'message' to either reinforce or challenge the voice of the curriculum. In addressing this matter, they have a twofold interest. On the one hand, they want to pursue the potential for new messages to counter a long established voice; on the other, they are aware of the potential for 'traditional messages' to deflect attempts to establish a new voice in and for physical education. As Penney (1998a) has highlighted in relation to developments in Australia, establishing a thematically based framework in policy documents is no guarantee of new emphases emerging in teaching and learning. So, what approaches, methods and pedagogical relations can be regarded as consistent with a 'critical pedagogy for social justice' and with the 'new voice' that they have proposed for the curriculum?

Specifically, they see a need for weaker framing (Bernstein, 1990, 1996) that is consistent with a conceptualisation of knowledge production as an ongoing and shared endeavour in education and that will facilitate the development of valued 'connections' between learning, and with more pupils' lives. Curricula would therefore need to feature less directive, more student centred and individualised teaching that facilitates creative roles in and approaches to learning.

However, Young has rightly pointed to the need to problematise concepts such as 'student centred learning'. They are prompted to take a more detailed and critical look at all teaching methods, and to be clear what learning students have been accorded a 'central role' in designing and developing, and whose and what interests are being advanced in this process. They emphasise a need for attention to focus upon the development of approaches that centre upon negotiation of experiences, but that also ensure relevance of these experiences for each and every pupil. They acknowledge that clear visions of such learning experiences are scarce.

In relation to these interests they draw attention to the value, but also some notable shortcomings in contemporary initiatives in physical education. Drawing upon Evans' observations, they contend that initiatives have essentially failed to '... presage the arrival of a form of practice which helps challenge either the hierarchies of knowledge or the social hierarchies which prevail inside the subject, within the broader work context and outside the school', such that '... the dominant concerns remain unquestionably ameliorative and hedonistic rather than socially transformative'.

Although Sport Education has been valuable in extending student roles, they do not yet know enough about students' views of these experiences and furthermore, see the model as failing to adequately embrace a socio-critical agenda. While Sport Education contexts may have seen the development of more democratic and equitable practices in schools, the tension that seems destined to arise between these practices and those beyond schools, where other discourses remain dominant, seems largely overlooked.

In advancing these ideas a useful framework to adopt as a reference point for the design of units of work and learning experiences, and for mapping progression in learning, may be one focusing upon what Engestrom has termed 'expanded learning'. Young explains that Engestrom's conceptualisation of 'expanded learning' comprises three steps in a cyclical process that progressively develops higher learning skills:

— the context of criticism in which the teaching and learning practices of the school are challenged and the tensions between a school view of the world as expressed in textbooks and the views expressed in the media and elsewhere are explored;

— the context of discovery in which new concepts are developed and used;

— the context of practical application in which new ideas are tried out in the real world.

— Inherent and explicit in these contexts is the transformative potential of physical education.

Index